CW00621684

RECONSTRUCTION
DECONSTRUCTION

DEMETRI PORPHYRIOS, HOUSE IN CHEPSTOW VILLAS, VIEW OF CONSERVATORY. SEE P 68

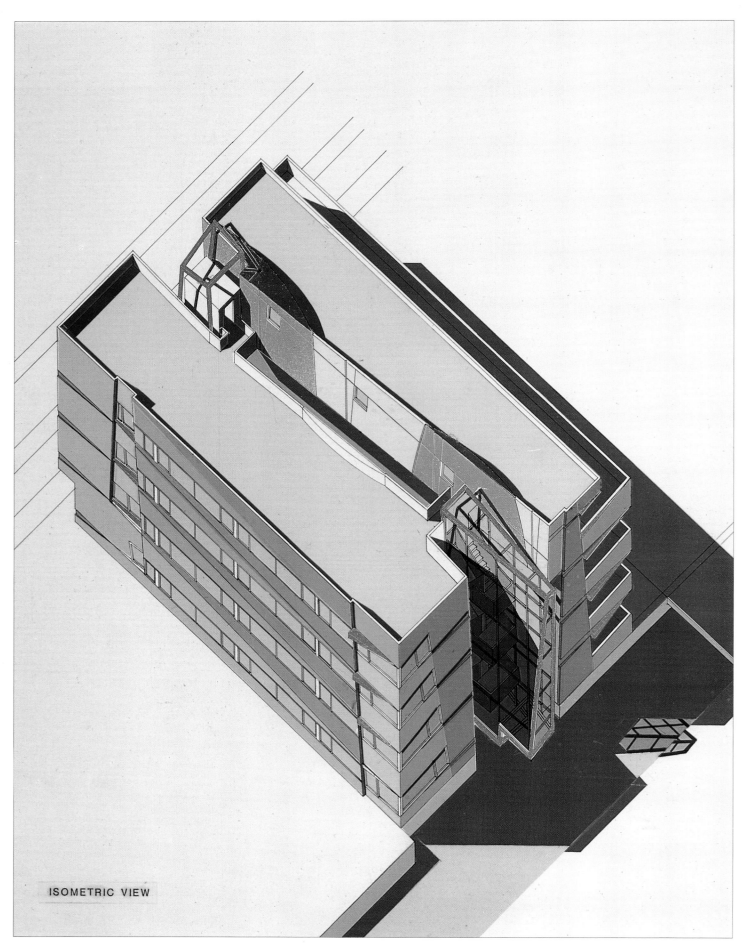

ISOMETRIC VIEW

EISENMAN ARCHITECTS, DEN HAAG HOUSING

An Architectural Design Profile

RECONSTRUCTION
DECONSTRUCTION

CHARLES SHOUP, HOUSE NEAR KORONI, ENTRANCE COURT STAIR, SEE P 76

ACADEMY EDITIONS • LONDON

Acknowledgements

The theme for this issue was suggested by Demetri Porphyrios to whom we are grateful for his help as indeed we are to Leon Krier, Peter Eisenman and to all the other architects who have supplied text and material

Photographs by Robert Oerleman of The Dance Theatre were specially commissioned by *Architectural Design*

We are grateful to Steven Brooke for the photographs of Seaside

Front Cover: De-collage of Leon Krier and Peter Eisenman projects; *Back Cover*: Seaside with view of Leon Krier's house, photo by Frank Martinez; *Inside Front Cover*: Bernard Tschumi, Bibliothèque de France; Institute for the Arts studio work; *Half Title Page*: Demetri Porphyrios, house in Chepstow Villas, photo M Fiennes; *Frontis*: Peter Eisenman, Den Haag Housing, photo D P Wilby; *Title Page*: Charles Shoup, house near Koroni, photo courtesy of Richard Economakis and M Lykoudis; *Contents Page*: Bernard Tschumi, Bibliothèque de France

Photographs: Peter Eisenman projects: Dick Frank and D P Wilby; Arquitectonica: Timothy Hursley and Paul Warchol; Demetri Porphyrios: Mark Fiennes; Andres Duany and Elizabeth Plater-Zyberk article: Frank Martinez and Steven Brooke

We are grateful to the Committee for the Preservation of the Acropolis Monuments for providing the material for the article on p47 and to Demetri Porphyrios for the photographs

Versions of *The Relevance of Classical Architecture* were read at the Classicism Symposium at the Tate Gallery, London (1988) and at Neocon 21, Chicago (1989). Photos supplied by the author

Traditional Towns is based on a lecture given at the Seaside Symposium, 1988

The City and the Classical Tradition is from a lecture given at Liverpool Polytechnic Student Symposium 1989

Editor: Dr Andreas C Papadakis

First published in Great Britain in 1989
New edition published in Great Britain in 1994 by *Architectural Design*
an imprint of the
ACADEMY GROUP LTD, 42 LEINSTER GARDENS, LONDON W2 3AN
MEMBER OF THE VCH PUBLISHING GROUP
ISBN: 1 85490 243 1

Copyright © 1994 the Academy Group Ltd *All rights reserved*
The entire contents of this publication are copyright and cannot be reproduced
in any manner whatsoever without written permission from the publishers

The Publishers and Editor do not hold themselves responsible for the opinions expressed by the writers of articles or letters in this magazine
Copyright of articles and illustrations may belong to individual writers or artists
Architectural Design Profile 81 is published as part of *Architectural Design* Vol 59 9/10 1989
Architectural Design Magazine is published six times a year and is available by subscription
Distributed in the United States of America by
ST MARTIN'S PRESS, 175 FIFTH AVENUE, NEW YORK, NY 10010

Printed and bound in Singapore

Contents

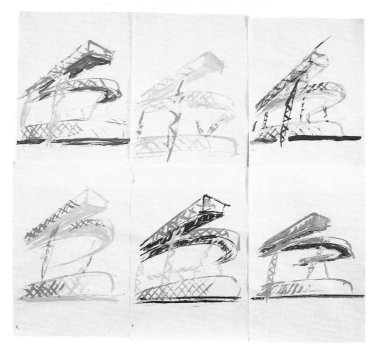

BERNARD TSCHUMI, BIBLIOTHEQUE DE FRANCE SEE P 34

PETRUM AMICUM APOCALYPS IS FORMAE

LK 77

LEON KRIER, NOTIONS OF CONSERVATION, 1977

PETER EISENMAN ▮▮ ▮▮ versus LEON KRIER

'My ideology is better than yours'

The theme for this discussion, held this year in Chicago, was conceived by Stanley Tigerman and reflects both the unyielding beliefs of two individual architects and the intense controversy between the fundamentally conflicting ideologies of Reconstruction and Deconstruction. Eisenman and Krier here debate issues such as the inexorable force of history, the question of universal values and the notions of presentness, tradition, modernity and change.

Leon Krier: Good afternoon, ladies and gentlemen. I think what finally constitutes the debate here is the conflict between architecture and anti-architecture. Is architecture still relevant or is anti-architecture a better expression of the mess we are in?

At present, lack of clarity in vocabulary, a confusion of terms and the widespread use of strictly meaningless jargon stand in the way of clear architectural and environmental thinking. The terminology used here is in itself sometimes an object of contention. I am therefore going to clarify some terms. The debate I think is between tradition, modernity and Modernism, and it is these terms which need clarification. I use the terms traditional and tradition in contradistinction to Modernism and Modernist; not in contradistinction to modernity. Yet at present, artists, historians and the public in general confuse the terms modern and Modernist. This is absolutely central. Modern merely indicates time and period, whereas Modernist clearly has ideological connotations. When historians write of the Modern Movement, they mean the modernistic movements as opposed to traditional movements. The traditional and modernity are therefore not contradictory notions. One can be a modern man of tradition. There is no contradiction.

Traditional cultures are concerned with the production of objects for long-term use. Modernist cultures by contrast are mainly occupied with producing objects for short-term consumption. These produce very different worlds for us to inherit or to live in. In such antagonistic philosophies, invention, innovation and discovery – and these I think are the central terms of this debate – have very different meanings. There is, of course, the claim that in a traditional culture you can't have innovation. But this statement is simply not true; it's mere slander.

In traditional cultures, invention, innovation and discovery are a means to improve handed-down systems of communication, representation, thinking and building. They concern not only art, philosophy, town building and language, but also the sciences, industry and agriculture. So they are a means to an end, mainly to conceive, realise and maintain a solid, lasting, comfortable and possibly beautiful common world. That is the goal. Fundamental aesthetic and ethical principals are considered to be of universal value and this is where the controversy lies; namely in the question of a universal value transcending time and space, climates and civilisation.

In traditional cultures, industrial rationale and methods are subordinate to larger themes, to larger concerns. In Modernist cultures, by contrast, invention, innovation and discovery are ends in themselves. It is claimed that constantly changing socio-economic situations constantly revolutionise our conceptions of the world; that there are therefore no universal ethical and aesthetic categories, and hence traditional values act as impeding and regressive straight jackets. In Modernist cultures industrial rationale and methods dominate; they are absolutely the most important features of life and they dominate all aspects of life: education, culture, recreation and so on. This I think is the central issue.

Peter Eisenman: The mistake that Michael Dukakis made when he ran for election against George Bush was that he allowed

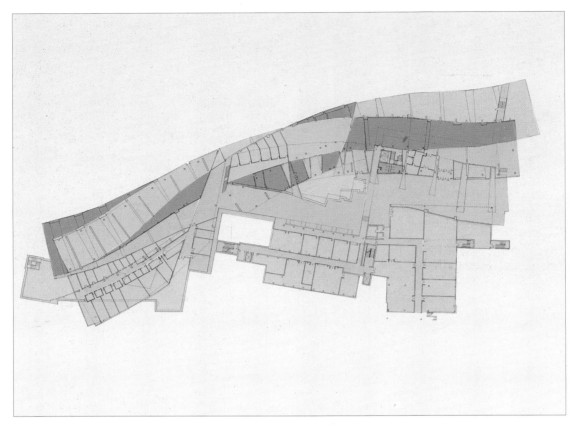

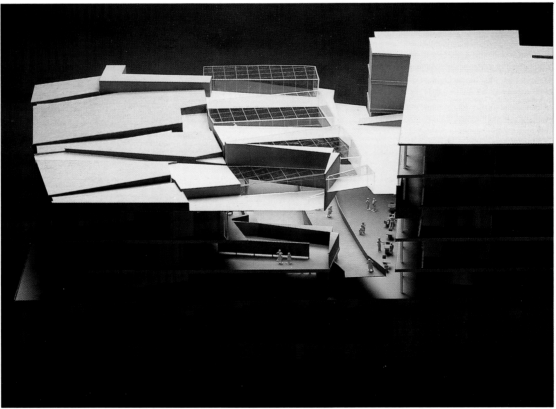

PETER EISENMAN, DAAP UNIVERSITY OF CINCINNATI, OHIO

The intention is to discover the building within the site. Its vocabulary will come from the existing construction; its chevron forms, together with the curves of the land, set up a dynamic relationship, organising the space between the two. It will challenge and change the mode by which we educate people; appropriate now that design disciplines have a far more important role in our age of information, more dominated by media than ever before. PE

Bush to paint the picture of Dukakis to the electorate. I agree with almost everything that Leon Krier has said. In fact it's difficult to *disagree* with anything that he says. Therefore, I'm not going to paint myself either out of or into Leon's picture. Rather I would like to present another picture.

The president of Princeton University recently said that the nature of the American university, particularly the nature of the private university, was going to have to change if Princeton was going to remain relevant to the education of the future leaders of our country. He said that it was no longer possible to maintain a curriculum with its basis in ethics, history, moral philosophy and the English language. He said that if America is going to produce world leaders it is going to have to train these leaders in the discourses that are relevant to today. He said that 80 per cent of the bills that go before Congress deal with some technological, scientific, sociological or other discourse, other than a humanist based one. He said that the students at Princeton were going to have to learn about ecology, environment, science and technology. They are going to have to do this, he said, in order to be able to deal with the issues that face the world.

I believe that architecture, and thus architecture curricula, are going to have to change to do this. It's no longer sufficient to be able to study the values inherent in the universal traditions that have led architecture into a condition of bankruptcy vis-à-vis today's reality. We all need tradition and monuments. But the nature of those monuments and traditions must change in relationship to the discourses which dominate our world today.

These discourses are different to what they were 500 years ago, 100 years ago or even 50 years ago. To remain relevant, every discourse must change. That does not mean that you abandon the tradition of that discourse. Rather it means to search in the tradition for what tradition in its very real sense always obscures.

The second issue concerns history. I believe that the Parthenon is a great building, a monument in the history of architecture. When I go to the Parthenon, I'm always moved by its condition; it is architecture but it is also part of history. It no longer has any relevance to building today; it has passed out of presentness.

20 years ago, when I went to Le Corbusier's chapel at Ronchamp, I was very moved by the experience and the sense of space. I thought it was a very *alive* building. Today when I go there, I feel it is now like the Parthenon; it has become part of history. I believe that the inexorable force of history erodes the presentness of the present. Architecture is always measured by how long it maintains its presentness as well as how long it survives in history. To build today does not mean to ignore the element of survival in history but rather to question how to maintain one's presentness. Therefore for me the Parthenon and Ronchamp, while monumental works in architectural history, no longer exert the same energy, because at some point they both passed out of presentness. I think architecture always deals with the problem of presentness.

The third aspect of the picture I am painting deals with building in reality. Both Leon and I have an ideological position. Leon draws architecture and I have to build it. There is a big difference between building and drawing. I am currently working on a 750,000 square foot convention centre. It is to be the new city hall, the new cathedral, the new place for convening in Columbus, Ohio. I was trying to think of ways to bring it down to human scale. I have a 700 foot long by 100 foot wide by 60 foot high concourse and the people who know about these things say you cannot touch it; you have to leave it alone; you can't do anything to make it more human or more humane. We don't need architecture. I have a hall that is 700 foot long by approximately 300 foot deep by 40 foot high that cannot be interrupted by anything but a column grid on 120 foot centres. I say to myself, on an $86 per square foot budget, what is it that an architect does?

Krier: I think that Peter's conception signifies the point of maximum entropy in architecture: turning architecture into anti-architecture. When Peter says that he's moved by the Parthenon, he's moved by a ruin. I'm highly irritated by the Parthenon as a ruin. For Peter, it seems to have no presentness, whatever that means, because he doesn't want it to be present. It doesn't fit into his picture. But there are many, many people out there for whom it is absolutely present. The great revolution of the American founding fathers lay in establishing the fact that different conceptions of the world can exist side by side, respectfully, and that the inexorable forces of history are not just on one line, moving in one direction, but that they change around. They can be changed by the sheer will of people and of individuals. I think it is terribly dangerous to submit oneself to the inexorable forces of history. And it's no good saying that you only have $80 per square foot. If this is the case, and you believe that you can't do a proper building for that, I think you should give up that building.

Eisenman: I only cited the Parthenon as an example, not because it is a ruin, but because I wanted, since it was a place of convening, to play it against the Convention Center in Columbus. When I went to Ronchamp 20 years ago, it was a vital building of *the now*. I felt it spoke to me of *the now*. When I went to it last year, I felt that it was about history and not about *now*. The difference between Ronchamp 20 years ago and Ronchamp today is that the culture has changed. It is inexorable, if only because then was then and now is now. And we cannot merely say that we are not going to build because conditions are not right.

Krier: It's not inexorable. It's what we want. Because if you say that the present conditions are inexorable, you always submit yourself to something you don't want and you look for an excuse to do something which you think profoundly isn't right.

Eisenman: Leon, let me propose something. What you mean by inexorable is this. I'm in a competition against Michael Graves. If I bow out, then Michael does the building. I profoundly don't want that. I don't think he's an inexorable force of history either. I at least have a chance to stand against Michael Graves and try for $86 a square foot, as he is trying to do. I don't believe that, as far as the condition of our contemporary public monuments is concerned – the shopping centres, for example, which are terrible places – we should just abandon them and the world as a whole and say that we are not interested; that we are only concerned with doing little houses and with building in fine materials. I think the task for architects is to provide environments that in some way confront the sensibility in which we live. I'm not saying that $86 is what I want, but right now I've got to prove that I'm worth more than $86 a square foot in Columbus, Ohio. I think that's the task. Not to say that I opted out.

Krier: One can be a modern man of tradition. There is no contradiction.
Eisenman: To remain relevant, every discourse must change.

Conservative versus Creative Restauration

Derelict Modernist Masterpiece

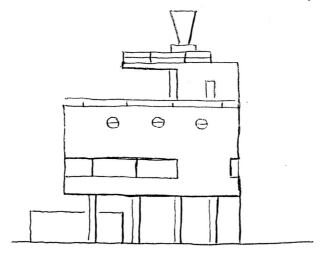

Conservative Restauration (Nostalgic)

Creative Restauration (Forward looking)

LK89

Krier: No, but we are not just talking about single building issues and single buildings. We are talking about fundamental terms of involvement. You yourself have much more ambition, I know, than just doing a single building here or there. Your buildings are statements about the way you see the world. We all know by now that the bankruptcy of our way of conceiving the world has to do with the short-term budgeting and too little money. So in the last 40 years we have been constructing public buildings, roads, industries and laying out suburbs on extremely tight budgets.

The maintenance bills of these shabby structures is haemorrhaging our private bank accounts and ruining our national balance of payment. If we take into account the long-term cost of a building and instead of wasting money in maintaining badly constructed buildings, we spend that money in solid initial construction, then we can afford the best building materials available. Now the problem is, I know, that you cannot go to the client and say I'm sorry but I have a long-term vision and you know at $86 per square foot, I can't do it. That is the problem facing the architect personally every day and there is little he as an individual can do. If however this problem becomes articulated by the profession it will become a point of policy. It will become part of a political discourse, and if that is so we will again be able to spend a lot more money now, in the present, to make buildings which are not just suffering from presentness but from everlastingness.

Eisenman: You and I both agree that architecture has got to become a political issue once again. You and I have no disagreement about that. The issue is that we are not training architects in our schools to deal with the political, environmental, social, economic and technological issues. We are still teaching them how to play scales. They are not adequately trained to deal with the power structure. We have bad architecture and bad cities because architects have been unable to provide solutions for those within the power structure, solutions that either speak to their needs or move them to understand that what they think their needs are, may not have anything to do with their *real* needs.

However, the real issue that divides us is what the nature of the public monument would be today, let's say, if we had the budget to construct public buildings. In other words, what would the nature of the monumental be? I would like you to say what you think it would be. If you think it would be a building from antiquity, because the monumental is always the same, then you and I have to disagree because I believe that the monumental is very different. We've got trucks, buses and 25,000 people coming to the doors of the Convention Center, and the scale of antiquity, the little camera art that you deal with, would not be sufficient to deal with so many people. We have to deal with them at a different scale and in a different way. But you say no.

Krier: We are talking not about matters of size but of morality. In any case, large crowds have been taken into account by architects for many thousands of years, whether they come by horse, cart, bus, or on foot; it does not change the problem fundamentally.

Eisenman: I didn't say that.

Krier: There are structures like the Colliseum which served very large masses of people.

Eisenman: But there is a very different relationship between leading an animal through a door and bringing a 20 ton truck through a door.

Krier: Yes, but you are not going to claim that your architecture is the way it is because you are bringing 20 metre long trucks through doors . . . The thing is presentness changes.

Eisenman: It does.

Krier: It is always changing. The aim of buildings is to last for a long while. Therefore, it must not only have presentness but something that is satisfying over a long period of time. This directly involves the idea of budgeting and the idea of aesthetics. Moreover it involves the idea of values and thecertainty which you have about those ideas.

Eisenman: Leon, the question of certainty went out of the window about 40 years ago. That's why you are slamming the table. It upsets you that it's gone.

Krier: That's your opinion.

Eisenman: It's not an opinion, but a fact. I suggested that there are two aspects of building, their presentness and their survival in history. Presentness can no longer be determined by certainty.

Krier: That may be your imperative. But that's not the truth.

Eisenman: I'm not speaking the truth. We are debating what we believe. Our ideologies are not necessarily the truth. There is no longer one truth.

Krier: If we can't comprehend it, it does not mean that there is no truth.

Eisenman: 2,000 years ago people believed the world was flat, even when Columbus set out to discover America. Truth changes in the course of history. History is a force which changes the notion of what is true at any one time.

Krier: You assume that those changes in the perception of the physical world, whether it's flat or round, imply that there are profound structural changes in the notion of morality.

Eisenman: Wait a minute. Who said anything about morality? You are introducing the notion of morality into the issue. I never raised that issue.

Krier: You may not have done so, but that is the issue.

Eisenman: You think the issue is that my buildings are immoral and your buildings are moral. Is that the way the debate has to go?

Krier: Yes.

Eisenman: Leon draws architecture and I have to build it
Krier: It is terribly dangerous to submit oneself to the inexorable forces of history.

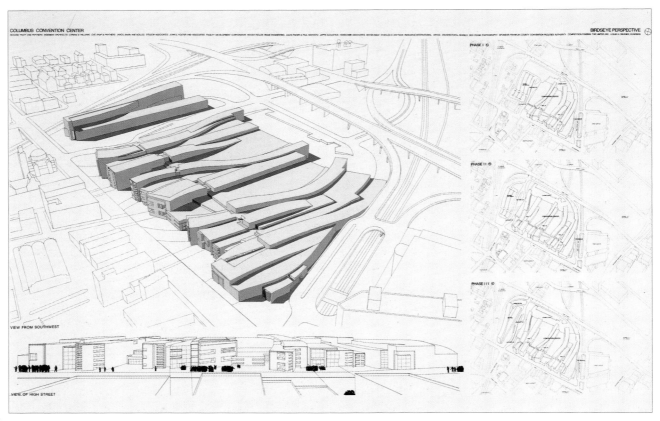

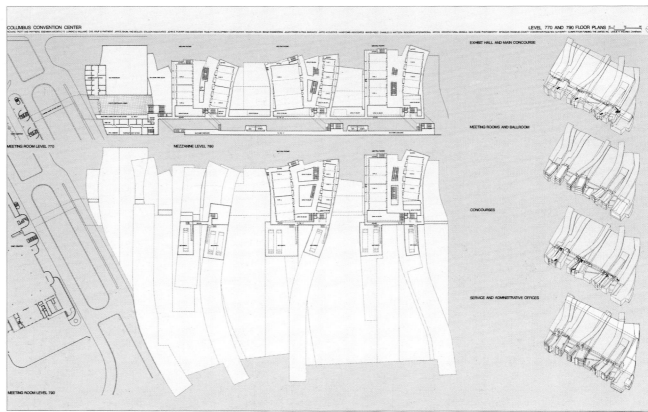

PETER EISENMAN, COLUMBUS CONVENTION CENTER, OHIO

In order to realise the vision for the Center and the City of Columbus, we adopted the theme that a convention centre was a place for convening, not a place to redeploy old conventions of architectural thinking in a new skin. The Convention Center should not be a conventional centre, but must go beyond being merely an amenity for a visitor, turning on and off according to the convention scheduling: rather it should enter into the daily life of the city as an ongoing participant and contributor. PE

Eisenman: Now we have a clear situation before us.

Krier: I think your buildings are cold. They are abstract. They are alien.

Eisenman: Since you've never seen one, I think you will be very surprised when you go to Columbus, Ohio. Certainly it's not an amoral building and I'm not an amoral person or an amoral architect and that's not the issue between you and me. Rather it is the nature of what signifies monumentality today, if one accepts a necessary separation between public and private building. The discourse is between a home and a public place of convening today. The issue is what the nature of a public place of convening is today. Is it a Parthenon or is it some other form of being? I think we have to look to other forms and other types to find relevant buildings for monuments and places of convening today. That is what the argument is about. You say we can look to history to find those types that exist. The Colliseum is there.

Krier: I did not say that. We don't have to look to history, but the harder we search the more we find that the fundamental types of spaces and construction have been known for a long while. They remain relevant exactly because they are timeless.

Eisenman: I maintain that if we look into history, we will find other types that have always been covered up by the architectural tradition. The tradition of history in fact covers up potential types which evolve today. For example, the shopping centre is not an historical type.

Krier: What about the bazaar?

Eisenman: Try to solve the shopping centre today in terms of the agora or the bazaar.

Krier: I'm talking about types of buildings which transcend styles and periods. The problem is that you claim that they are a part of a history and that that history is past.

Eisenman: No. I'm saying that the solution to the problem of the shopping centre may lie in what history has covered up; not in what we see in history but what we have not seen in history.

Krier: You mean history has been covering up.

Eisenman: It's like searching for gold. We know it's there in the ground but we have to find it. Within the architectural tradition that you speak of are relevant forms that we can only see today because the lens of seeing has changed.

Krier: I claim that it hasn't changed, because if it had changed, the cities and buildings of the past would be for us absolutely, utterly and totally irrelevant; yet you very well know that they are not. They are in fact the most desirable places to live. In order to be relevant in whatever one does as an architect, one must know how our buildings fit in the larger picture of the town, the landscape, the world. Every architect, whether he wants it or not, is a system builder or a system destroyer because every fence, every telephone box, every piece of plaster that he puts on the wall fits into a picture of the world. There are no excuses for

subjecting ourselves to the 'inexorable forces of history' if we know that those forces threaten our sanity and lay our planet and our societies to waste. The fact is that people either convene or they isolate themselves. These are the truths of the human condition. There are grand buildings for a lot of people to meet and there are modest buildings for people to isolate themselves. There are places where we behave as citizens and places where we behave as private people.

Eisenman: It is the nature of what grand means today. This room we are in has no sense for me of being grand. 50 years ago it may have been thought grand. It is the Grand Ballroom in one of the grandest hotels in a grand city. But I would not design a room like this today as a public place of convening. It would be very different. I'm not suggesting that we don't need public places for convening or that there is no difference between public and private. What I *am* saying is that there is no universal nature of the grand; the terms have changed. The terms of universal value and certainty have changed. It doesn't mean that there is a change in morality. It means that the notions as to what constitutes certainty, proof, grand, monumentality and public places of assembly have changed. We as architects have got to find other solutions because if not, people are going to continue to find themselves existing in the atopias of modern-day shopping centres. We think these are not problems that architects should be dealing with. But it is precisely these problems that architects should be confronting; problems of places where people actually convene today. If we are not satisfied with these places we have to find ways of changing them. What is at issue between us, Leon, is what that means today. We have no models for they are.

Krier: I think that the problems are not only problems of appearance but rather problems of a fundamental nature. We are not going to improve our ecological and social conditions by making more Peter Eisenman-like convention centres and shopping centres. That can't be the issue of architecture.

Eisenman: You always personalise the issue.

Krier: Well, it is a personal debate. Isn't it?

Eisenman: I never say we are not going to make the world any worse by making Leon Krier buildings. I don't feel that. I think we need more Leon Krier buildings.

Krier: The fact is that you constantly say that the conditions have changed. The conditions for airports, for example, may have changed and may require development or perhaps the discovery of building tasks which are still obscured by history because they were of no use in the past. That is where invention is possible. Now, as far as the American house is concerned. You drive across this country and 99 per cent of the houses which people think of as houses are traditional homes. You know that. There are bad traditional homes, good traditional homes, brilliant homes, perfect, dreadful, sad. But they are really all traditional homes. Now that is the free market where people are actually free to choose. Why do they choose traditional homes? Because they think that home, the place to raise a family, is what generally everybody understands as a traditional home. Condi-

Eisenman: We cannot merely say that we are not going to build because conditions are not right. Architecture has got to become a political issue once again.

OVER-development of CENTER
UNJUSTIFIABLE PROFIT - MAKING

Urbanization of SUB-urb !
JUSTIFIED PROFIT MAKING

FUNDAMENTAL CHOICES OF URBAN DEVELOPMENT

tions have not changed in the way you present it.

Eisenman: We don't live in homes that are being designed for people today. We need a new type form of home; the type form that talks about families that live in two different cities, that have two working people in the family, so that nobody is at home taking care of children during the day. Such a type form does not exist. A whole different structure of home is necessary and if we continue to build whatever your notion of a home is, and this has changed over the centuries as you know, then we will not solve the problems. The form of house has constantly evolved. We as architects have got to propose a new form of home, because the old forms, whether the Palladian villa or the Leon Krier form, don't work any more, for a middle-class family without servants.

Krier: They do work. They still do work. They may be comfortable, bad, mediocre or brilliant. But they still work and they still correspond to what most American people understand as homes. That is not the problem. They are full of innovations.

Eienman: They correspond to nostalgia.

Krier: They are of our time. The problem is not for us architects now to propose completely unseen forms of home which would fit this changing alien condition of people being divorcees, children running away and being punks and so on, but of improving that material which is commonly understood to be 'home'. The problem is not the way the home looks or the way it is organised. That problem is largely solved. The problem is how most homes relate or don't relate to the town. It is first of all a town-planning problem and to that Modernists have no theory and no solution which can be taken seriously in the long-term perspective.

Eisenman: How can you sit here with me and say that the problem of the house is solved? It's this notion of certainty which you have that I find staggering today.

Krier: It is staggering isn't it.

Statements made in response to questions from the floor:

Eisenman: We measure buildings by two standards: how long they maintain their presentness and how long they retain themselves in history. Some buildings both lose their presentness and never go into history. I believe buildings can have presentness for 50 or 100 years. I'm suggesting now that I no longer feel a presentness in Ronchamp. I just about feel a presentness in James Stirling's Leicester Building, which I used to feel enormously. I feel no presentness in Stirling's Tate Gallery.

*   *   *

Eisenman: I wasn't talking about validity. We were talking, as Leon said, about personal feelings. Each of us, I think, when we go into a building, feels whether that building is part of history. We feel moved by it because of its history or we feel moved by it because it is speaking to us about the present condition of humanity. I'm suggesting that certain buildings speak to us about

the present condition of humanity and certain buildings speak about history. I'm not suggesting that I am the judge of that, nor should Krier be. Each person has to decide for him or herself.

*   *   *

Eisenman: Presentness. What is that? I think it's different for each individual. I went to see Rem Koolhaas' Dance Theatre in the Hague and I was struck by its presentness. There was something about it that moved me. I don't know what it was. I could probably sit down and quantify it today. How long it will last I'm not certain. What I *am* certain about is that there are very few buildings that I would say have presentness. I think Aldo Rossi's Gallaratese had it when I first saw it; I am less moved by its presentness today. Presentness is a concept that fascinates me. I am struck by the fact that every time I go and see Michelangelo's Lorentian Library it never loses any quality for me because it never had anything but that quality. There is something that happens in one's relationship to a building, something that causes presentness to change. I believe it is subjective.

I love the same buildings that Leon likes, but I do not love those same historical buildings being constructed today. For example, I profoundly objected to the rebuilding of the Barcelona Pavilion. I found that it had no presentness at all; it was like Disney World. It is rebuilt but it is not the same. I don't believe it now has anything to do with presentness. I believe that it belongs in history and when it was built I'm certain that it had incredible presentness. There's no sense in rebuilding it today. For the same reason, I believe that to construct any of the buildings that would be models for Leon's discourse, they might have an enormous sense of history but in a very different sense than presentness.

Krier: I think that the problem is an absolutely reverse one because buildings of the past can only be relevant to us today if they never had presentness at all but rather a spirit of all time because it is this which gives it relevance over a long period of time. So if a building has this strange presentness today, tomorrow it will be passé; it will just be for our time and will therefore be irrelevant tomorrow.

*   *   *

Eisenman: The only university course that I teach right now is one on Palladio. Palladio interests me because it's a subject that is never mentioned in any of the literature that comes out of Leon Krier's historicism for the reason that Palladio was a Modernist.

Krier: I agree, in so far as he was anti-conventional in his use of building types.

Eisenman: There is something in the work of Palladio, the invention of typology, that intrigues me, the invention of a social typology and a building form that were dislocated from the works of the time. We are still building Palladian villas. Our shopping centres are basically the same villa type expanded with great green lawns around them. We have not gotten away from the villa type. The pervasiveness of this type in history interests me. It has enormous presentness today because it has become a pervasive building form. The transcendence of the periphery, the

Krier: A building must not only have presentness but something that is satisfying over a long period of time.
Eisenman: Presentness can no longer be determined by certainty.

15

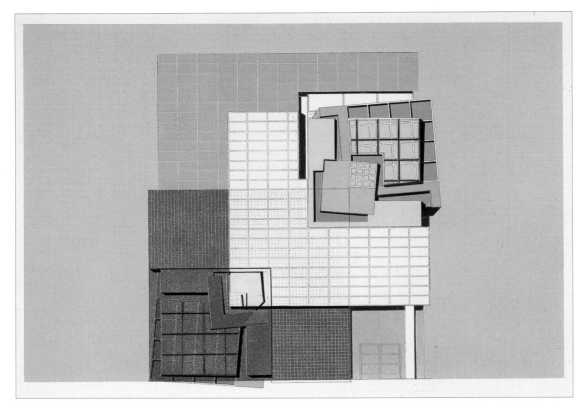

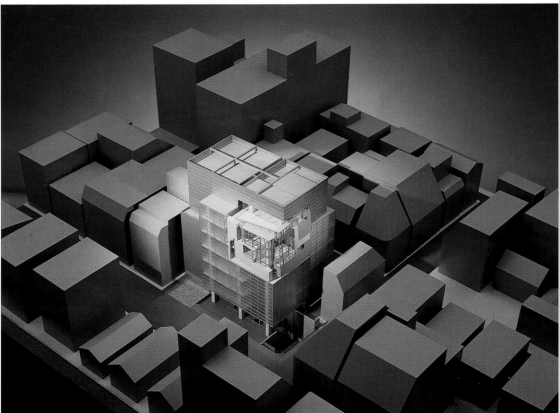

PETER EISENMAN, KOIZUMI SANGYO BUILDING, TOKYO

The model and elevation show a building which was inspired very much by Tokyo itself, which seems to the Western mind to be a 'place of no place', an atopia. The idea of atopia has always been a part of the Japanese language itself: the word *ma* is the notion of a space betwe; *ku* means no place. Thus the idea was not to build a *place*, but rather a *place between*. The project deals with the manifestation of this 'between' by exploring the idea of imprint and trace as records of past and future development. PE enclosure, the frame of building, are enormously important and these reach a point of clarity in the work of Palladio.

So I look at Palladio not in terms of Palladio himself but rather to question what it is about the type form that has enormous presentness today. That is why I teach Palladio. I find it interesting that Palladio is repressed for some reason by the Post-Modernists. He is not a subject of the discourse of Post-Modernism. They skirt around him. The argument that Tafuri makes is that at any one time in history there is always one architect who is looking forward and one who is looking back. At the time of Alberti and Brunelleschi, Brunelleschi was looking forward and Alberti was looking backward. Alberti introduced the subject of the Classical typology whereas Brunelleschi introduced an invention from science called perspective. If we had not had a Brunelleschi, that is somebody looking outside the discourse into what might be possible, we might not have had perspective. We, sitting at this table today, are Alberti and Brunelleschi. Leon is certainly Alberti. I aspire to being Brunelleschi. I'm willing to stand on that discourse; the difference between the two.

Krier: But you cannot pretend that Brunelleschi was a break with history, which is something you promote.

Eisenman: I'm not a break with history.

Krier: You are the culmination of history then.

Eisenman: No. I'm saying that Brunelleschi went outside the discourse of architecture and looked at what it was in fact repressing at the time, and opened up the discourse. Alberti returned the discourse to the past. That's the difference between us, the difference at any time in history. I'm within the architectural tradition but I'm in the Brunelleschian tradition rather than the Albertian tradition and it's never going to change. I'm not saying that I don't respect Alberti. That's why we are here.

Krier: I recently saw a programme on television by Richard Rogers who walked through buildings of Brunelleschi implicitly claiming that he was obviously the new Brunelleschi. There are uses and abuses of history.

Eisenman: Please don't bring up Richard Rogers because that just throws us into another area.

Krier: There is an affinity in both your uses of history.

*　　*　　*

Eisenman: If you took a student, a first year student who had never heard of Mies van der Rohe, to the Barcelona Pavilion today and said here is what presentness is, I don't believe the student would find it, because of where the world is and the culture that the student lives in; the training he has had; the way he uses language; the way he sees; what television has done to this student; what simulation has done; what film has done, etc. All of these discourses have bombarded him in such a way culturally that he can no longer see the way Mies van der Rohe saw in 1929; it is virtually impossible. Therefore, to recreate the Barcelona Pavilion, to have someone look at it and see within it

the spirit of 1929 or what it signified at that time, is an impossibility. We have got to change if we are going to remain relevant. Discourses lose their relevancy. For example, the study of Greek has lost a certain relevancy today. We must respond to the conditions of today in order to remain relevant as architects. That does not mean rebuilding Mies van der Rohe's Barcelona Pavilion or anything like it.

Krier: Peter always talks about things having changed. The conditions have changed. Everything seems to have changed. Yet people don't change biologically.

Eisenman: Psychologically they do and have.

Krier: How do you know?

Eisenman: How do you know they don't? You are always certain. Let me be a little certain. Freud seems to think that people do change and evolve psychologically.

Krier: Yes, Freud did. If things have changed so radically and if architecture should be affected by that radical change, why does aeroplane design, or car design not change?

Eisenman: Did you say that aeroplane design has not changed?

Krier: No. The planes still have two wings and motors.

Eisenman: They used to have six wings.

Krier: Yes, but that is not the change you are talking about. You mean that they shouldn't have wings or they should have wings funny ways up.

Eisenman: Rockets don't have wings.

Krier: That's why they are called rockets.

Eisenman: They are still aircraft.

Krier: But of a different type. Heisenberg's uncertainty principle applies to the sub-atomic level only. It does not change our understanding of the apple, or the right-angle, or the aeroplane.

*　　*　　*

Krier: If you fill a position of authority and you are supposed to teach architecture you'd better be certain of what you are teaching. Otherwise, there is no place for you as a teacher. Otherwise, you have a faculty of doubts, not of architecture.

Eisenman: I absolutely disagree with Leon that you can't have a curriculum and a faculty full of doubt. Leon would have a curriculum and would force people to teach it. I'm interested in people who doubt because that's the only way you are ever going to change and remain in any significant discourse.

*　　*　　*

Eisenman: I think the Convention Center will be the monument

Eisenman: Truth changes in the course of history.
Krier: Your buildings are cold. They are abstract. They are alien.
Eisenman: I'm not an amoral person or an amoral architect.

17

of today. Every city is going to have one. It's the way people are going to meet, the way business is going to be done and we had better find a way to solve the problem of monuments and the need for them today. I think it's very different from the need in the19th century or the 15th century for a monument.

*   *   *

Krier: Instead of quarrelling about presentness, we ought to be talking about how, as architects, we can spend limited resources and time in an ecological and aesthetic way. Some architecture magazines and schools may be absorbed by revivals of Modernist stylisms, but that is an irrelevance to the building market. It is irresponsible to day-dream in the face of the colossal ecological and social problems which Modernist planning and industrialism cause. Modernism provides no solutions to those problems, because it is itself an integral part of those problems.

Eisenman: What you forget all the time is that zoning ordinances are written by people, people in a political process within a democracy, and they are voted on by people. You seem to think that these people are either uninformed or that you know better than they do. If you do then it is incumbent upon you to get into the political process and try to effect that change in those designing ordinances. I suggest to you that the zoning ordinances are not necessarily always as ruthlessly out of touch with what you see to be an urban order. I suggest that they represent some other kind of interest that you seem not to agree with.

*   *   *

Krier: Unless zoning ordinances, planning and building briefs are radically rewritten, architects can do nothing but contribute to the ecological holocaust which is now under way. I am now planning a small town in Dorset where most urban functions will be integrated within a 5 minute walking radius.

Eisenman: The town that Leon is designing, as opposed to a place like Tokyo, has no sense of what urban order or structure is today. I would like to argue that Tokyo is a fantastic model of urban order. It has less crime than any other major city yet it is a passionately urban place which follows none of the rules of hierarchy of grand alleys, vistas, structures of buildings, materials, or scale, that Leon is going to have. Urbanity has many different forms. If we only think of the form of an 18th-century town then we are going to continue to have the kind of repression that exists in the notion of a Classical architecture.

*   *   *

Eisenman: As I was preparing for this debate there was only one book that I thought it necessary to read and that was Nietzsche's *Thus Spoke Zarathustra* because it is a book that both Leon and I understand very well and it probably brings us very close together. I believe that it was on page 61, (although I'm not certain as I didn't bring the book with me. I don't like reading from prepared script because I respond to the presentness of this

situation) but it was something about the creator. What Nietzsche says is that the creator is a lonely person and must always stand apart from and perhaps against the mass, and will always be in a sense outside and alien to the existing order. In that sense, I guess that I agree with Leon that the creator must have a degree of certainty to do that. I think that Nietzsche then asks the question, how does one have the right to be a creator? In other words, how does one have the right to sand outside? What is that right that allows one to arrogate to one's self that possibility?

My answer to that question is that people who are not creators don't think about that right. They remain within the mass always. I don't think we are talking today about the monument, history, morality, etc. I think we are talking about those individuals, architects sometimes, poets, physicists, whoever has had that need to stand outside and therefore the right to stand apart. To be those wanderers who always understand what presentness is because the need for creation is always involved in presentness. Great architecture, I would argue, has never been liked by the masses. The great monuments always have been, in their time, not necessarily liked or understood. We do not know, when we build today, whether we have either caught the spirit of our time because it's an elusive thing; nor whether we catch the presentness or whether we are building, as Leon said, in the spirit of all time. I think it's the willingness of the creator to take that risk; the risk of being alone and of attempting to define that elusive condition. That is what makes an architecture of presentness.

*   *   *

Krier: There is a sad, melancholic ring to all this. Peter may be right. Many ecologists believe that it is too late to save the planet, and Peter's tortured buildings express the dissoluteness we are in. Maybe his buildings will be the homeopathic poison able to revive our healing capacities, and will strengthen our resistance to decay and decomposition. I doubt it. Melancholy is with us and the inexorable fate of mankind seems to be to lay waste this planet as soon as possible. Therefore some people think that if we waste energy, it should be to our own satisfaction. That, however, is the central paradox, and therefore I am ending with another dogmatic statement, if you don't mind.

The symbolic poverty of current architecture and townscape is a direct result and expression of functional monotony as legislated by functional zoning practices. The principal modern building types and planning models such as the skyscraper, the Groundscraper, the Central Business District, the Commercial strip, the office park, the residential suburb etc, are invariably horizontal or vertical *over*concentrations of single uses in one urban zone, in one building programme or under one roof. Uniformity of use (functional monotony) faces even the best designers with a limited choice between either the expression of true uniformity or that of fake variety. Blandness or kitsch, artistic cruelty or caricature are the almost inevitable result.

The *symbolic richness* of traditional architecture and the city is based on the proximity and dialogue of the greatest possible variety of private and public uses and hence on the expression of true variety as evidenced in the meaningful and truthful articulation of public spaces, urban fabric and skyline.

Eisenman: I love the same buildings as Leon, but I do not love the same historical buildings being constructed today.
Krier: Buildings of the past can only be relevant today if they never had presentness at all but rather a spirit of all time.

DECONSTRUCTION

  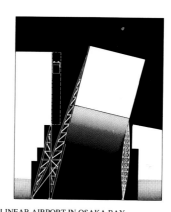 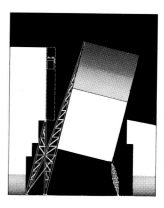

BERNARD TSCHUMI, A 21ST-CENTURY LINEAR AIRPORT IN OSAKA BAY

These diagrams illustrate sections along the linear city. The unusual location on an artificial island suggested a bold move on the part of the architect: to look at the airport as the generator of the ultimate linear city and a 24 hour line that would conceptually extend around the globe, a relentless sequence of events. Such a programme required a powerful image that would challenge all architectural preconceptions about structure and composition.

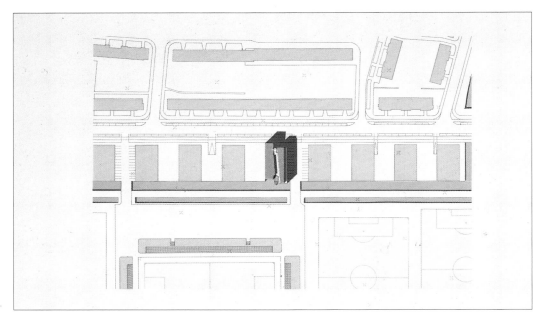

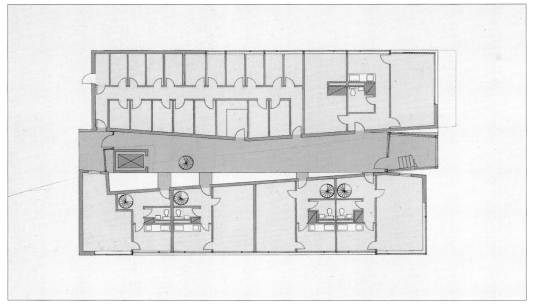

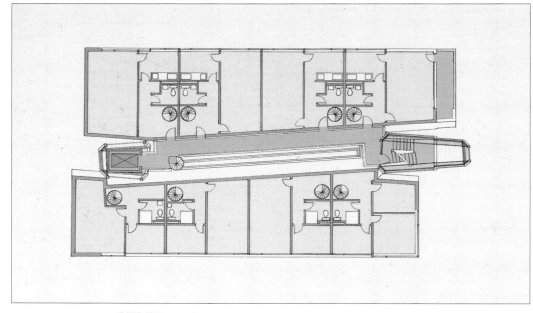

ABOVE: SITE PLAN; *CENTRE*: FIRST-FLOOR PLAN; *BELOW*: FOURTH-FLOOR PLAN

PETER EISENMAN
Recent Projects

MODEL

The Hague Social Housing
The 200,000th Home Housing Festival

The Hague City Council with the Office for Metropolitan Architecture has organised a special Housing Festival to mark the completion of the 200,000th home in this city during 1989. A linear site along the Dedemsvaartweg will display every conceivable housing typology from an isolated single family house to a multi-apartment tower.

The project was conceived in order to explore innovative ideas in the living space in the city. It encouraged architects to break new ground in this area specially neglected during the years of fast and massive reconstruction in Europe after the War. Eisenman Architects was selected in March 1989 by the Festival organisation to design a 17-apartment 'Urban Villa' and to meet the challenge of creating a radical design within a restricted social housing budget.

Eisenman Architects have explored a new concept of the Urban Villa by generating a central public circulation space as a sequential progression of three-dimensional dislocations of the same absent space. This erosion splits the building into two independent, 'sheering', living blocks.

The building is the receptacle of the imprints of the passage of this conceptual eroding of voids. Left inside the new gap are 'Trace Frames', narratives of the stationary which overlap the voids. Going home becomes a new experience, one of a recollection of events, a sequential reading of traces of the dislocation of time and place.

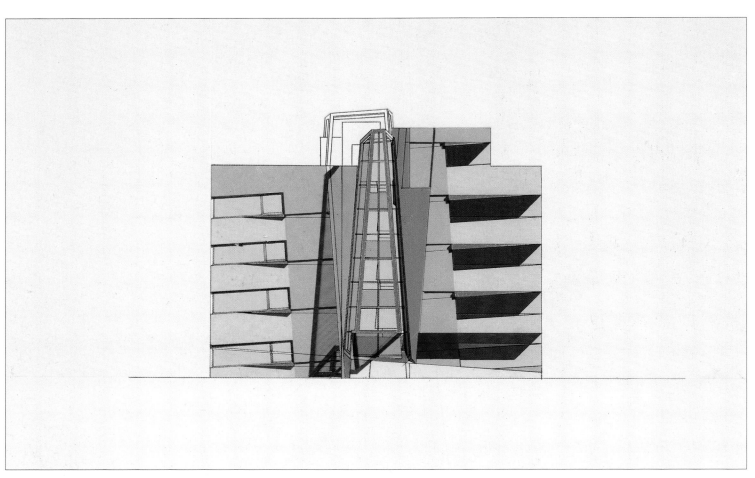

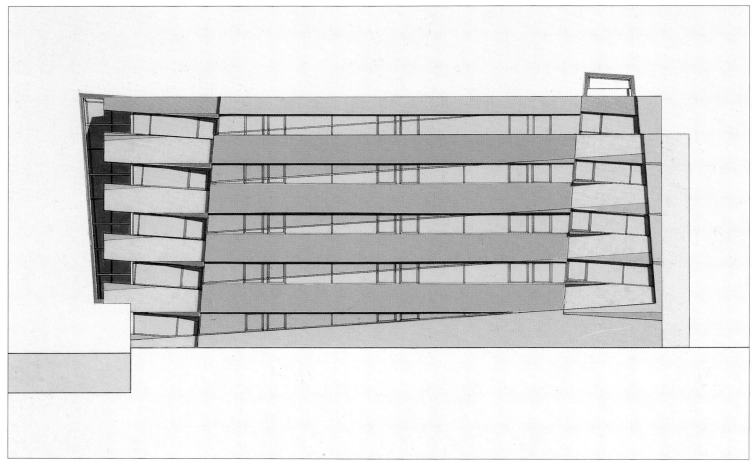

ABOVE: SOUTHWEST ELEVATION; *BELOW*: SOUTHEAST ELEVATION

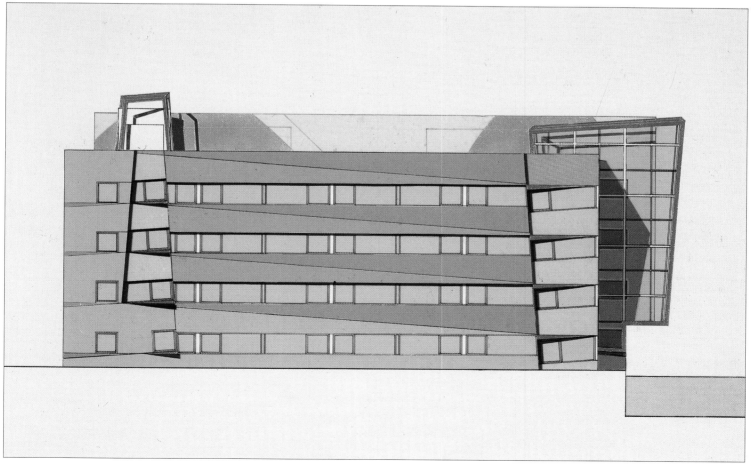

ABOVE: NORTHEAST ELEVATION; *BELOW*: NORTHWEST ELEVATION

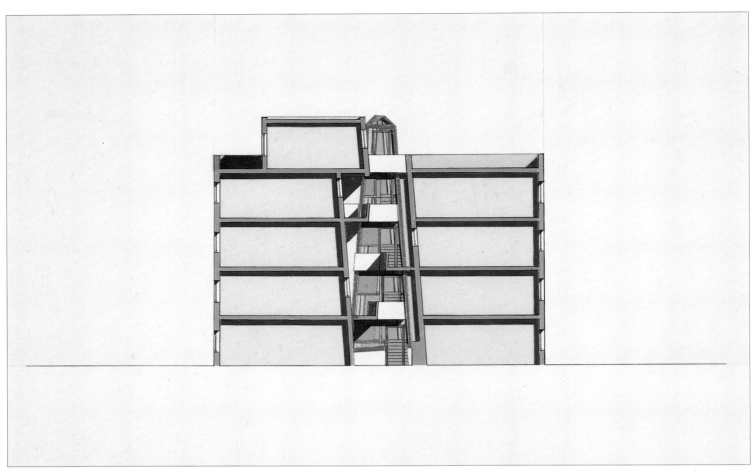

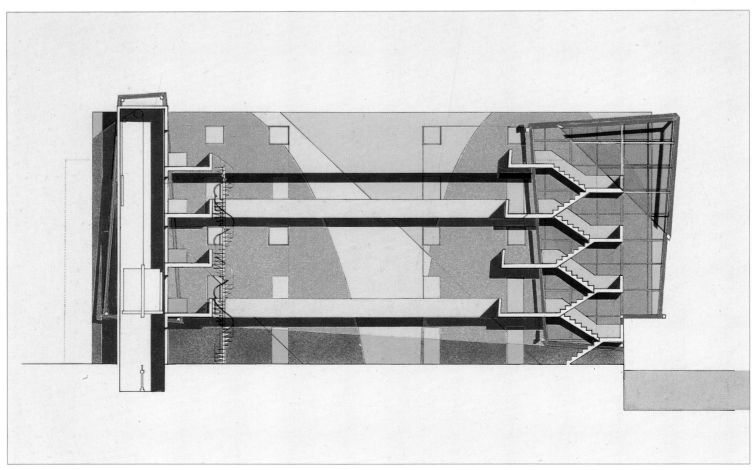

ABOVE: CROSS SECTION, SOUTHWEST VIEW; *BELOW*: LONGDITUDINAL SECTION, SOUTHEAST VIEW

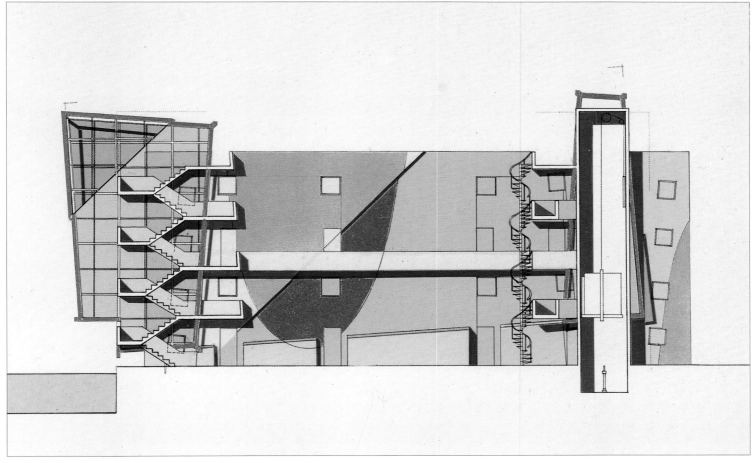

ABOVE: CROSS SECTION, NORTHEAST VIEW; *BELOW*: LONGDITUDINAL SECTION, NORTHWEST VIEW

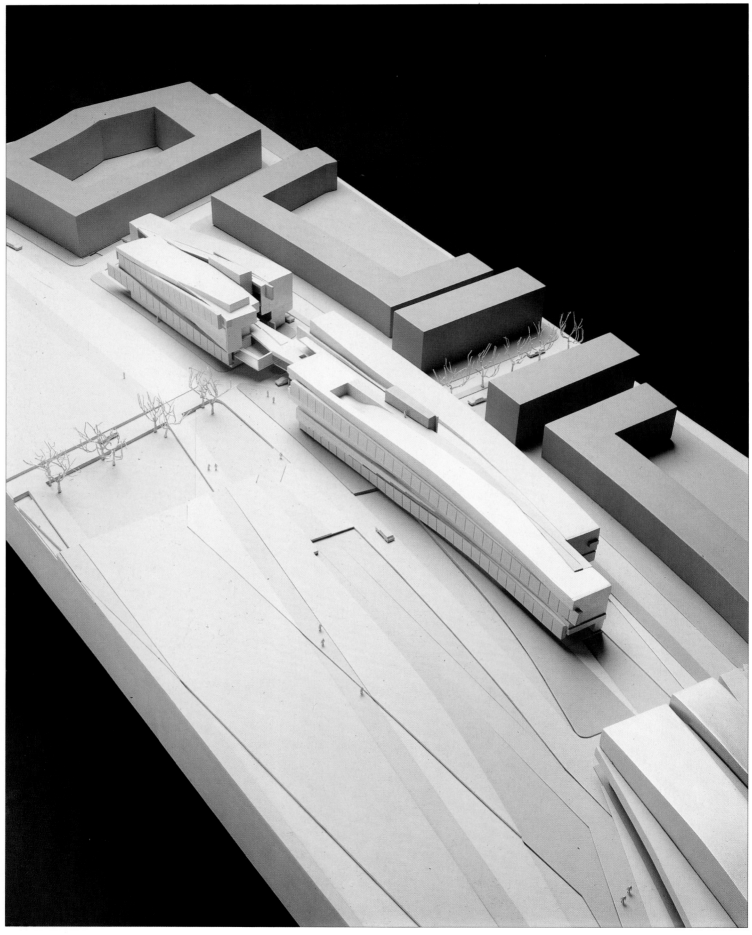

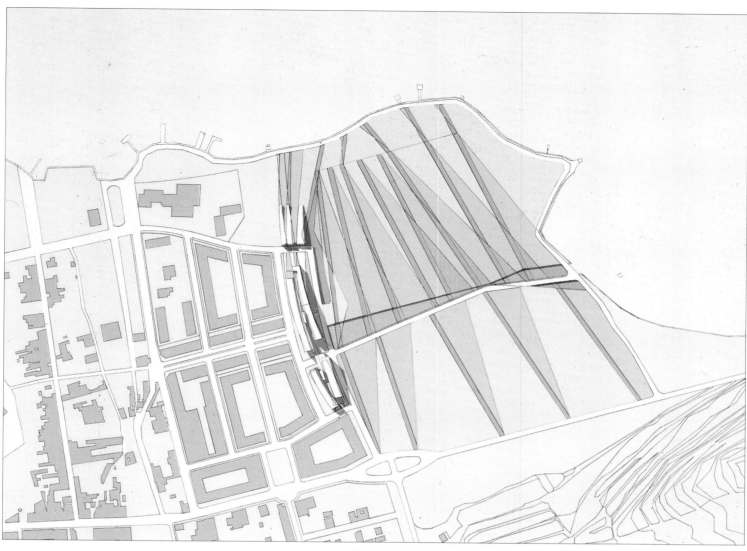

SITE PLAN

Barcelona Hotel Competition

Our society has lost contact with reality. The media has been able through sophisticated techniques to simulate reality to such a degree that we often can no longer tell what is real and what is not. It has been able to capture reality through the use of simplification and reduction – iconic, strong, forms – for example, the now omnipresent logo. Architecture was traditionally the domain of reality – bricks and mortar, house and home. Now it too has become threatened by the mentality of the media. Architects have begun to design the image of their buildings and not their buildings; they design for the single photo, the magazine cover. This further dilutes the reality of architecture. In order to recover reality architecture must displace itself from the media, begin again to find its own discourse. There are two major displacements which can be sug-

gested for architecture. The first is from the design of necessity to the necessity of the arbitrary; the second is a shift from primary, strong form to secondary weak form.

Media is design. Architecture was traditionally the design of necessity; the mediation of function, structure, meaning and even form itself in form. But there is another condition of necessity which is potentially as important for architecture (and which has been repressed by the Classical conventions of ordination and design); this is the necessity of the arbitrary. It is quite different from the necessity of function.

It says that what is random, chaotic, disorganised contains a necessity as equally compelling as the necessity of rational function. The random thus is only random in light of Classical Order. When

this is stripped away, another even more powerful necessity can be found. Thus design as we know it represses the arbitrary, and in a certain way the necessity or the arbitrary is opposed to design.

The displacement of necessity to the arbitary also leads inevitably to conditions of secondarity or weak form. Secondarity in this sense does not mean to suggest a hierarchy or a dialectic with the former metaphysics of the primary. Rather it is to suggest that in the primary there is always a repressed condition of the seondary, and equally in secondarity there will always be repressed conditions of the former primary.

Displacing these repressive conditions opens up the possibility of other conditions of form and image. Since what is being displaced is primary strong form, what naturally will accrue is something

27

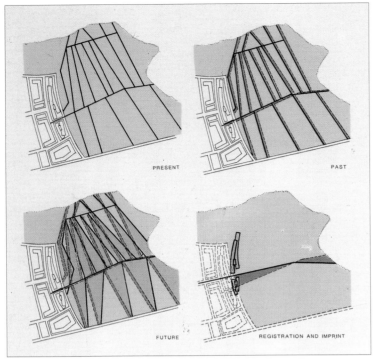

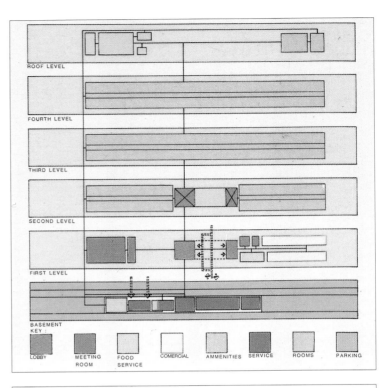

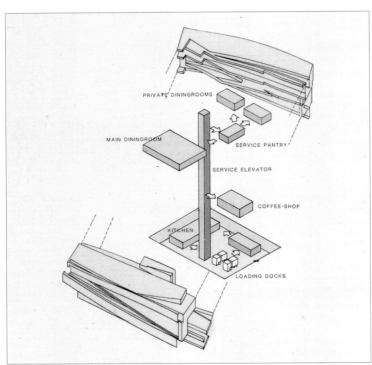

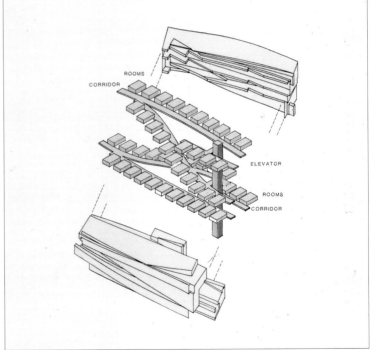

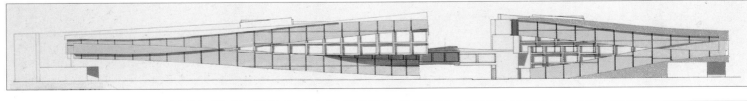

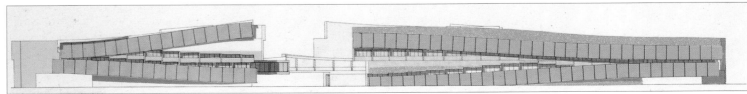

ABOVE L TO R: CONCEPTUAL DIAGRAM, FUNCTIONAL DIAGRAM; *CENTRE L TO R*: FOOD SERVICE DIAGRAM, ROOM ACCESS DIAGRAM; *BELOW*: SOUTH AND NORTH ELEVATIONS

EXTERIOR ENTRY PERSPECTIVE

less monolithic, less contained, less building like in the traditional sense.

These displacements manifest themselves in our project for Banyoles. The building is no longer a primary form – a single metaphysical enclosure. The line of its geometry (necessitated by the repetition of seemingly like units) is no longer Cartesian – that is everywhere the same at any section along its length (the definition of a Cartesian line).

This produces a building of incredible richness and complexity while at the same time preserving the simple autonomy and replication of bedroom units but it is also a building which is not a building in the traditional sense but is also part landscape. Equally the landscape becomes part of the displacement of the building. It exists as three different trace conditions of

time – the trace of time past as represented in the form of the agricultural divisions that existed around the turn of the century; the trace of time present in the extension of the building form into the landscape and the trace of two notions; one where the agricultural divisions and the building divisions become the arcs of the sweeps of an eight-oared shell; the other is the sliding of the divisions backwards as the sliding of the seats of the shell backward as the shell skims forward. Here then is a condition of both secondarity and the arbitrary as projected into a displaced building/landscape. Because of these displacements from 'primary' building and 'secondary' or supplemental landscape a new secondarity becomes. The resulting form and space no longer can mean in the conventional sense of architectural mean-

ing, but also displaces these meanings from the primary conventions of architectural meaning. Thus it is not possible to look at this building and ask what it means. In this sense it means nothing. But because of this meaning nothing, another level of potential significance – previously repressed by conventional meaning is now liberated. Equally the 'interior' space of the building is no longer merely the static lobby – corridor – room stacking of the traditional hotel. Instead there is a sliding and a slopping found in the possibility of the form of the line which creates another condition of interior/exterior space.

Thus this project then not only symbolises the spirit of new Spain in the world of 1992, but also the new world of an architecture possible for the 21st century

29

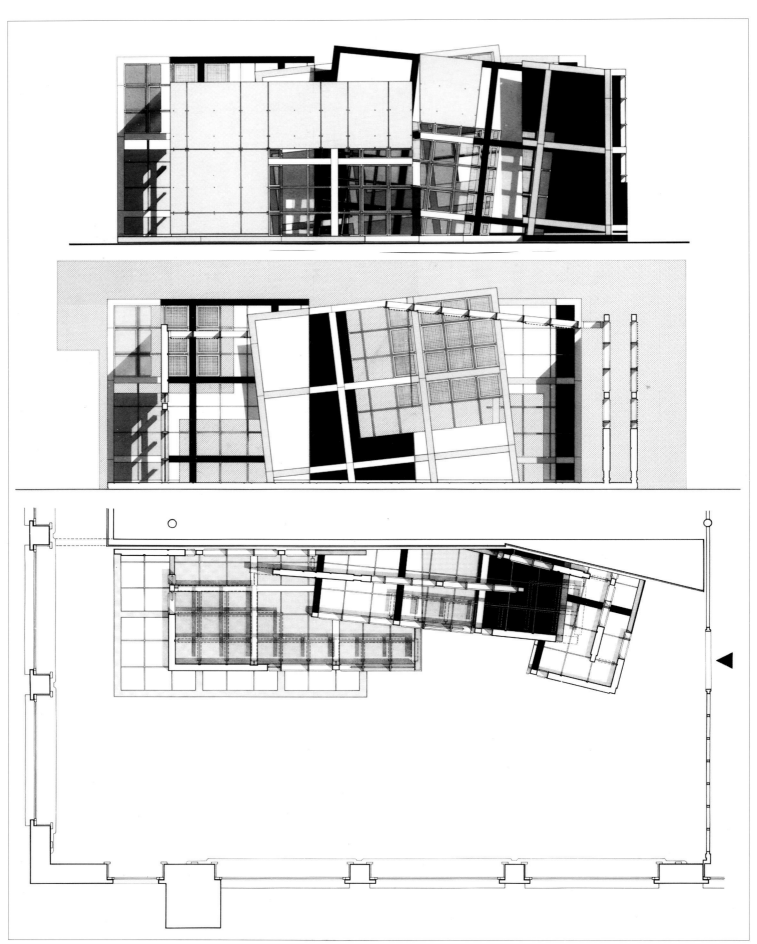

ABOVE: ELEVATION; *CENTRE*: SECTION; *BELOW*: PLAN

HIROMI FUJII
'The Nave of Signs'

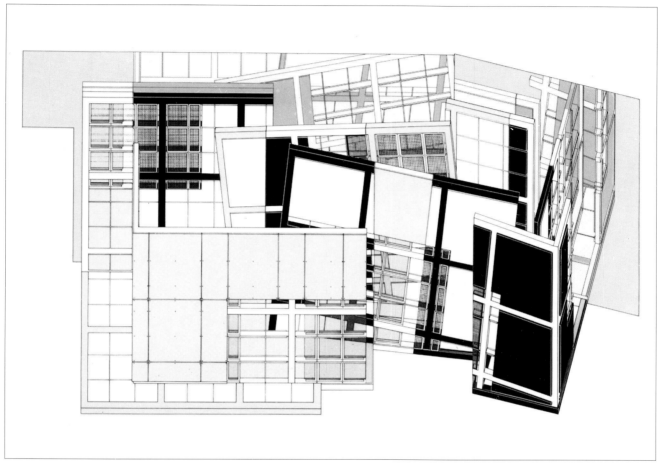

AXONOMETRIC

This project is being entered in the Europalia Exhibition to be opened in Belgium this October. At the same time, it is a model of the concept behind my recent works.

The theme of the exhibition is how matter is transfigured and becomes architecture; ie the emphasis is on transfiguration.

My intention was to express in a concise way the transfiguration of not only material or form but the compositional system of architecture; ie its structure. I selected metal as the material that was to be transfigured; similarly I chose the cube as the structure that was to undergo transfiguration.

This metal cube is gradually and repeatedly segmented, divided, and compressed, producing a dispersed space of layered fragments. In order to inscribe the segmenting, dividing, cutting, detachment, and layering of space, I began by using grids and colours as signs of traces and then generating in them, differences. The grids and colours, which are traces, induce mental operations such as suppression, displacement, and reversal, make perceptible the presence or absence of things and the basic states of things such as reality and fiction (positive and negative), and inscribe spatial events such as segmenting, dividing, cutting detachment, layering, and dispersion. This space is thus composed of elements that are related by means of mental operations in the depths of the consciousness.

Compared to spaces that are integrated in a centralised manner through surface mental operations, this project at first glance may seem diffuse and dispersed. However, by introducing as the basic compositional language of this space those marginal elements that hitherto have been deliberately discarded because they were not thought capable of being coordinated or integrated, such as the unconscious or the mental operations of the consciousness – ambiguity, diversify, and polysemy, it was intended to create a new spatial structure (ie compositional system) able to deal with diverse and complex conditions.

Trans by Hiroshi Watanabe

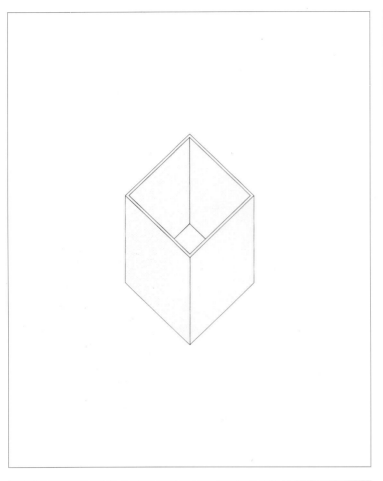
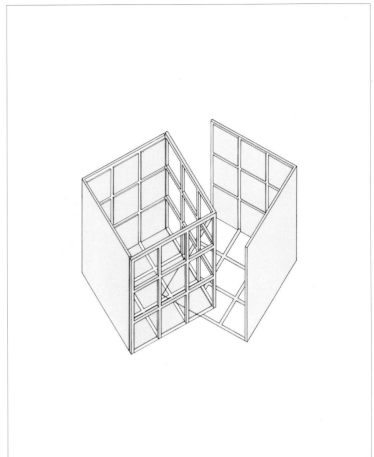
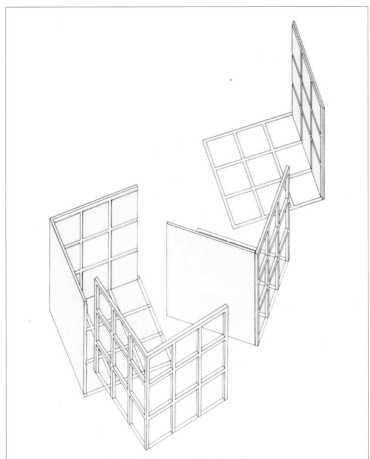

ABOVE L TO *R*: PROGRESSION AXONOMETRIC I & II; *BELOW L* TO *R*: PROGRESSION AXONOMETRIC III & IV

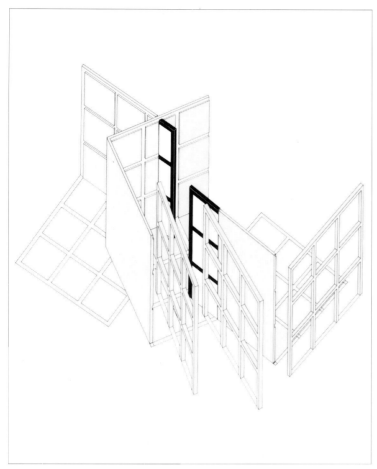
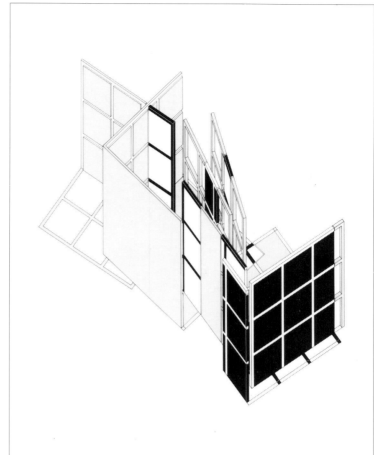
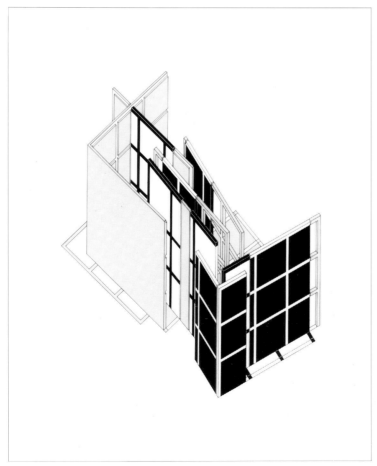
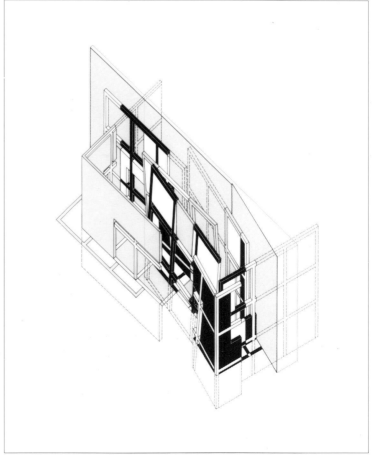

ABOVE L TO *R*: PROGRESSION AXONOMETRIC V & VI; *BELOW L* TO *R*: PROGRESSION AXONOMETRIC VII & VIII

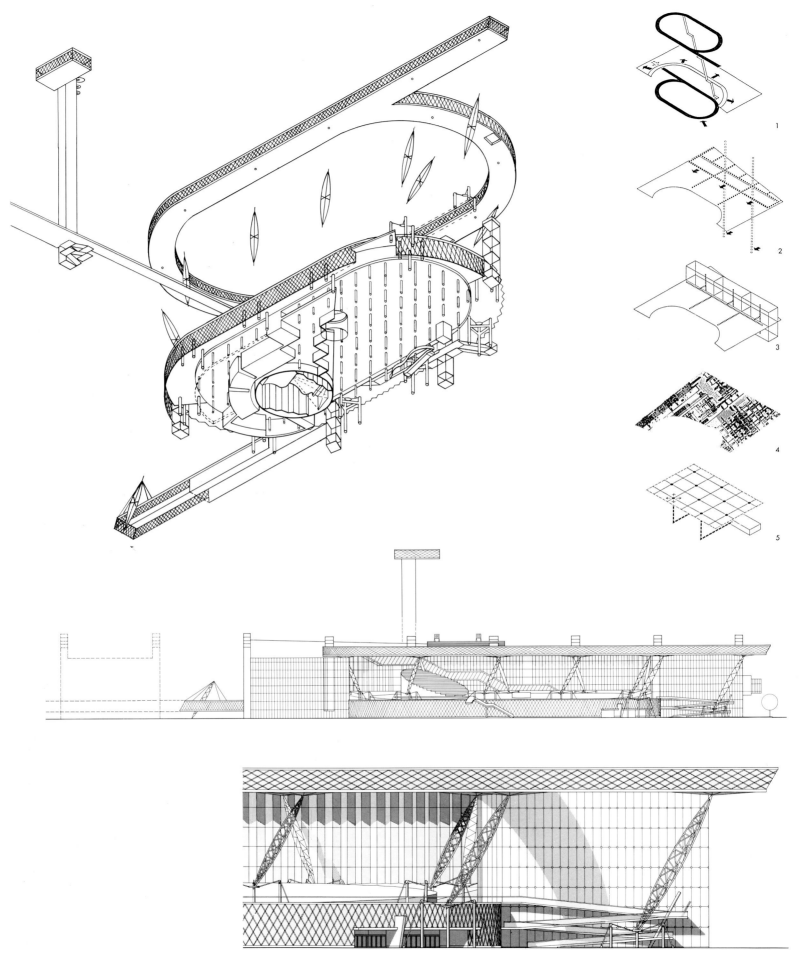

ABOVE L TO R: PARTIAL EXPLODED AXONOMETRIC; DIAGRAM SHOWING LAYERED CIRCUITS; *BELOW*: ELEVATION

BERNARD TSCHUMI
Bibliotheque de France

PHOTOMONTAGE OF SCHEME

This is a new type of library combining the pursuit of modernity with the pursuit of knowledge; the athlete with the scholar. Opening simultaneously onto the Seine, Paris, Europe and the rest of the world, it enjoys at the same time, internal 'circuits' of library culture. The building will act as an urban generator of a new area of the city. Inside there are multi-media 'circuits' for the public, circuits for the books and visible architectural circuits of the most up-to-date information technology. A main 'circuit' offering both excitement and architectural permanence, is combined with reading 'trays' offering maximum flexibility.

The fact that the library is not located in the historical centre of Paris is considered to be an important and positive factor. Its very eccentricity allows it to break away from static concepts of libraries. It is not a frozen monument, but must instead

be turned into an event. Hence the concept of open circuit, where the endless pursuit of knowledge is matched by the pleasure of physical effort. Locating a running track over the library is more than a dynamic convenience, it embodies the library's complex role as the generator of a new urban strategy (the open circuit).

Within the new library, five interrelated sets of circuits can be identified: The visitors' and administrators' circuits, the book circuits, the electronic circuits and the mechanical circuits. While each circuit has its own logic and its own set of rules, the circuits interact constantly at strategic locations.

In order to comply with the inevitable evolution of the programme, first during the planning stages, then over many years of use, we have devised a free and flexible system of 'trays'. By placing public circulation on one side and storerooms on the

other, we have obtained the free space on the 'trays', only rhythmed by the grid of structural columns and the grid of stairs & HVAC.

Throughout the history of architecture, some of the most significant works have been library programmes, for example, those of Boullée, Labrouste, Carrére and Hastings, Asplund and others. The new library should be compared to such illustrious precedents even though nostalgia for outdated spatial forms should be avoided. We have therefore, displaced the traditional central reading room towards the exterior. The space of the Great Hall inside and Esplanade outside, is the revolving circuit of the project.

The Architects have searched for dynamic circuits of the future, whereby the concept of library revolves around movement: movement of people and movement of ideas.

ABOVE: VIEW TOWARDS EXHIBITION SPACE;*BELOW*: VIEW OF LIBRARY

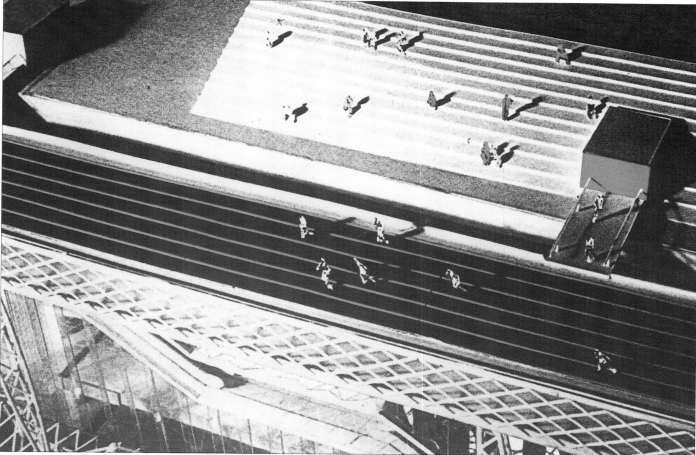

ABOVE: VIEW UNDERNEATH EXHIBITION SPACE; *BELOW*: VIEW OF RUNNING CIRCUIT

SECOND FLOOR LEVEL OF ENTRANCE FOYER

REM KOOLHAAS – OMA
The Netherlands Dance Theatre, The Hague

EXTERIOR VIEW FROM THE PLAZA

The Dance Theatre is part of the larger Spui complex which also contains a hotel, Concert hall and the future city hall all sharing a plaza in the centre of the Hague. The formal facade reveals nothing of the interior, where colourful planes and abstract shapes elegantly collide.

An entrance foyer on three levels has the dynamic spatial quality conveyed in a Koolhaas painting. The theatre itself has an auditorium which seats 1001 and a Proscenium stage for dance and opera. There are technical facilities and accommodation for the Dutch Dance Theatre. In addition offices, costume ateliers, three rehersal rooms, green room, sauna and pool are provided. There is an inverted gold cone which marks the entrance and the restaurant.

The theatre itself is constructed from steel beams and girders, using metal cladding with sheet rock covered with stucco, marble and gold foil. There is a special emphasis on the use of colour in the interior which contrasts with the more sombre exterior shades of black, white grey and metallic.

L TO R: ENTRANCE FOYER: EXTERIOR VIEW

ENTRANCE FOYER SHOWING THE THREE LEVELS

ENTRANCE FOYER FROM THE THIRD LEVEL

ENTRANCE FOYER

ABOVE: STAGE AND AUDITORIUM *BELOW*: WAITING AREA ON GROUND FLOOR LEVEL OF ENTRANCE FOYER

ELENI GIGANTES AND ELIA ZENGHELIS
Moabiter Health Forum, Berlin

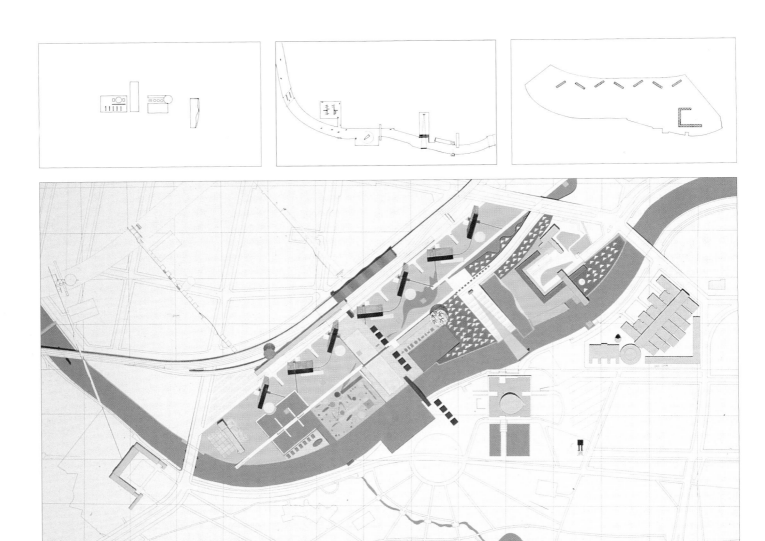

ABOVE: CONCEPTUAL DIAGRAMS, *L TO R*: ARTIFICIAL WATER FACILITIES; RIVER ACTIVITY; BUILDINGS; *BELOW*: PLAN

The challenge of the brief is to create a new metropolitan resort for Berlin, while interlocking Moabit with the Tiergarten and the rest of Berlin, reversing its isolated 'island' character.

The design was conceived as a sequence of overlapping and interlocking 'teeth' (programmes); the Tiergarten invading the New Park, the New Park biting into the Tiergarten, Moabit occupying the New Park and the New Park flowing into Moabit; the design exploiting the presence of water as the material available with which to develop the idea.

Moabit is characterised by the architecture of large utility objects freely disposed in space, a condition impossible within the tight fabric of the old city. This creates its own tissue which, together with the dominant combinations of infrastructure (trains, boats, roads etc), gives it a dramatic metropolitan condition waiting to be activated.

This project proposes that the Moabiter Werder Park be developed as a new kind of 'spa'. The entire site is conceived as a 'Health Forum' – a symmetrical counterpart to the Kulture Forum across the Tiergarten – where the actual use of the site relaxes the body and mind. It is conceived as a 'vale of health': hydrotherapy pools form a path in the gardens, threading through botanical aromatherapy arbours, while a small clinic is supplemented by whirlpools, plunge pools etc, culminating in water aerobics jutting into the river.

The S-Bahn Station adds to the drama of the location. Apart from acting as the entrance to Moabit and the spa, it has a symbolic presence. We propose to combine it with a wax museum of figures from Berlin history – a long beam suspended over the tracks – and a global planetarium which can double up as a 3-D cinema.

A total of 581 apartments are divided between seven slabs along the rear of the site. The apartments, varying in size, are interchangeable and can be redistributed in different combinations per slab. All variations can be accommodated within the same structure. Raised on piloti, and floating like large canvases, these slabs provide an urban edge to the Tiergarten and the beginning of Moabit.

ARQUITECTONICA
Banco de Credito, Lima, Peru

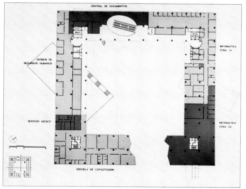

ABOVE: VIEW OF EXTERIOR; *BELOW L TO R*: FIRST FLOOR PLAN; SITE PLAN

The corporate headquarters for the largest private bank in Peru, on a site of 530,000 sq ft, is located at the foot of the Sierra outside Lima. The four-storey building consists of a broken courtyard raised on white marble piloti, surrounding an Inca burial ground and ruins.

Recalling the traditional Spanish-Colonial courtyard model, with a formal public facade on the exterior, and a more informal interior facade, it is also a modern design. Piloti support a free-form interior plan, together with user spaces on the roof, sculptural facade elements, and a free-flowing terrain below.

Various forms are situated underneath, including the bank, cafeteria and auditorium whilst others such as the lobby and board-room slice through the structure. These forms are clad in white marble and stucco. An elliptical entry space intersects the building vertically and is made of glass blocks surmounted by a skylight. The exterior facade consists of strip unmullioned windows of blue glass and diagonally-mounted indigenous black marble. By contrast, the interior facade of the broken courtyard is made from locally quarried pink slate stone, cut in 'natural', irregular slabs and the fenestration is of green, tinted-glass squares laid out with irregular spacing.

The layout ensures the high degree of security required for this type of construction. Public entry is possible only through the ellipse form and all other ground-level facilities perform public functions, not directly attached to the building above.

All the interiors are designed with special orientating features such as cylindrical elevator lobbies and zig-zag glass-block walls. The finishes, carpets, panelling, and much of the hard furniture, including special desks, credenzas, and the systems office furniture, have all been designed by the architects, using local craftsmanship and colours derived from traditional Inca palettes.

Principals: Bernardo Fort-Brescia, Laurinda Spear; *Project Architects*: Martin J Wander, Enrique Chuy; *Project Team*: David Di Giacomo, Bill Holt Jr, Ziyad Mniemneh, Richard Perlmutter, Janice Rauzin, Fernando Villa

RECONSTRUCTION

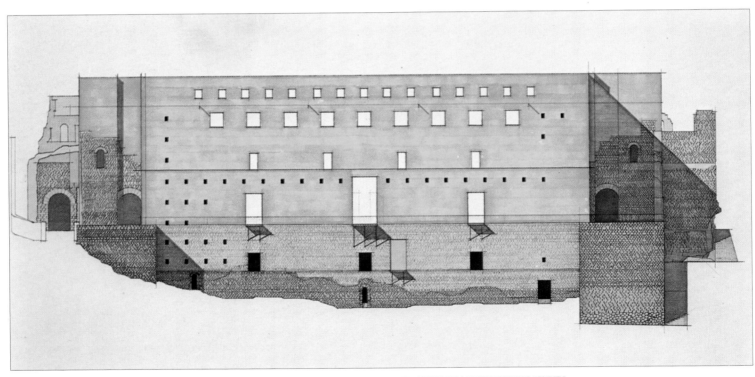

GIORGIO GRASSI, THE ARCHITECTURAL RESTORATION OF THE ROMAN THEATRE IN SAGURITO
The theatre at present has, to a large extent, the appearance of an artificial ruin as what is most evident to the visitor is the more recent efforts at a rather unfaithful restoration of the Roman structure. Giorgio Grassi envisages the reconstruction of those essential parts of the theatre's structure that are necessary to convey a clear idea of the architectural space of the theatre in its entirety.

Reconstruction of the Acropolis Monuments: 1975-1986

ERECHTHEION

For almost two and a half thousand years, the Acropolis monuments have been exposed to the ravages of time, which along with natural and war disasters, have given rise to serious problems in recent years. The critically dangerous state of preservation was noticed for the first time during the 1940s. Specialists first became alarmed on observing cracks and fractures on the surface of the marble. During the following years, drastic deterioration

and the precarious nature of the situation were repeatedly documented in reports drawn up by experts and finally in a report drawn up by specialists in Unesco in 1971. The Acropolis Ephoria under the Ministry of Culture attempted to deal with the most imminently threatening dangers using the limited technical and financial resources at their disposal. By 1975, however, it had become evident that there was a need for a conservation project on a grand scale involving decisions and operations far exceeding the responsibilities and capacities of the Ephoria. The Ministry of Culture, therefore, founded the Committee for the Preservation of the Acropolis Monuments, made up of scholars, archaeologists, architects, civil engineers and chemists, whose job it is to prepare studies, set up the programmes, and to supervise and carry out the operations required to preserve the Acropolis Monuments. The first permanent members of the Committee include the present chairman of the Committee Charalambos Bouras, professor at the National Technical University; George Dontas, Ephor of the Acropolis in 1975; the late John Travlos, the memorable investigator of Athens; the chemist Theodore Skoulikides, professor at the National Polytechnic University. The first chairman of the Committee was the late John Meliades followed by Nikolaos Platon and George Mylonas. The Committee also includes members of the Ministry of Culture such as the director of the Department of Antiquities and the director of the Department of Restoration.

The years 1975-1977 were primarily devoted to preliminary studies. The problem relating to the Acropolis Monuments were documented and studied in depth. The main causes for the

deterioration of Acropolis Monuments are, firstly, the rusting iron clamps used for restoration in the 19th and 20th centuries and the pollution which has increased in the last 30 years, causing damage due to physical, chemical and biological changes in the surface of the marble. Other problems are the static sufficiency of the architecture and the wearing away of the rock floor under the tread of thousands of visitors.

In 1977 the first phase of the project came to a close with the publication of the 'Study for the Restoration of the Erechtheion' which presented a detailed analysis of the state of preservation and formulated proposals on ways of dealing with the problems. These proposals took into account the international guidelines concerning restoration set forth in the Charter of Venice in 1964 and also introduced other guidelines called forth by the unique nature and artistic value of the monument. In December of 1977 Greek and foreign specialists unanimously approved this report at the International Meeting on the Restoration of the Erechtheion and praised it as a 'model for future restorations'.

In the course of its long history the Erechtheion has been subjected to many changes in both form and function and has suffered severe damage. The building was partly destroyed by a conflagration in ancient times. It was heavily repaired in the Roman period, later converted into a three-aisled Christian basilica, used as living quarters and as a powder magazine during the period of Turkish rule, then reduced to a ruin in the beginning of the 19th-century.

The first attempts to rebuild the temple were carried out directly after the Greek war of Independence. In 1839-1843 parts

EAST PORTICO OF PARTHENON, RECONSTRUCTION DRAWING

ABOVE: DETAIL OF PARTHENON; *CENTRE*: DETAIL OF ERECTHEION; *BELOW*: RECONSTRUCTION OF PILASTER, ERECHTHEION

L TO R: PARTHENON: PORCH OF CARYATIDS, ERECHTHEION

of the north, south and west walls were rebuilt under the direction of K Pittakis who used scattered architectural blocks of marble for the purpose. In 1846-1847 the French architect Paccard restored a fragmentary caryatid found in the excavations and reset it in its original position. A copy of the Caryatid was set up in the place of the one which Lord Elgin had removed from the building together with other architectural members.

From 1902 to 1908 N Balanos carried out a major reconstruction project which gave the Erechtheion the form it was know by until recently. The following parts of the building were restored using both original material and, to some degree, new material: the ceiling of the Caryatid Porch, the ceiling of the North Porch, the south wall up to the height to the crowning moulding, the west wall up to the height of the cornice and a large part of the north wall.

In 1975, the Ministry of Culture and Sciences founded the Committee for the Preservation of the Acropolis Monuments responsible for organising and supervising the studies and works on the reconstruction of the monuments.

The restoration of the Erechtheion began in 1979. A Papanikolaou, architects, K Zambas, civil engineer, and Mrs M Brouskari, archaeologist, were in charge of the work. Professor Ch Bouras of the National Technical University of Athens G

Dontas and the late J Travlos supervised the project on behalf of the Committee for the Preservation of the Acropolis Monuments. The Caryatids were transferred to the Acropolis Museum. During the following years all of the sections of the building which had been restored by N Balanos at the beginning of the century were dismantled: the south wall as far as the orthostate course; the ceiling of the Caryatid Porch and the crowning moulding of the parapet supporting the Caryatids; the west wall as far as the course below the attached columns; the ceiling, cornice blocks and some of the frieze blocks of the North Porch; the north wall above the doorway and the remaining section. The building had to be dismantled in order to remove the iron clamps. The blocks and other architectural members were treated where the rusting iron attachments were removed and replaced with titanium. Where statically unsatisfactory, ancient blocks were pieced together with new marble. The broken surfaces of ancient blocks are highly irregular and in the old days the restorers used to even out the surface in order to have a tight join with the new piece. In order to avoid disturbing the ancient blocks, a pointing device was used to create the reverse of the old broken surface on the new marble.

Two basic restoration principles were laid down by the Acropolis Committee: a) titanium was used to attach the old and

L TO R: PARTHENON; ERECHTHEION

new marble pieces; b) other fragments were cemented together under pressure, using white cement purified of all sulphur compounds. Once treated the blocks were reset on the building. Some of the architectural blocks that had been wrongly reset in previous restorations have now been restored to their original positions in the building.

In 1981-1982 a small-scale conservation project was carried out at the Propylaea. In the East Porch the second architrave from the south and the neighbouring blocks were consolidated.

The Acropolis Committee did not limit its concerns to the great monuments only. In 1978 a pathway was constructed for visitors on the Propylaea-Parthenon axis. The rock slopes of the Acropolis suffer from erosion causing landslides and the breaking off of large boulders, and in 1977 the work of consolidating the rock began.

The 'Study for the Restoration of the Parthenon' by the architects Manolis Korres and Charalambos Bouras came out in 1983; a comprehensive work dealing with the history of the building, its architecture and its technical features. The study included proposals for the restoration of the Parthenon in 12 programmes: the four sides of the colonnade, the north and south flank walls, the east and west porches, the *pronaos* and the *opisthonaos* the platform with the steps and the floors.

In September, 1983, the 'Study for the Restoration of the Parthenon' was presented to an international conference of specialists held in Athens. The first programme concerning the restoration of the east front of the Parthenon was unanimously approved and work started in April 1986.

So far the raking cornice blocks at the southeast and northeast corners have been taken down and also the pediment *simas* and the lion head spout at the northeast corner. The conservation is carried out at the work site of the Parthenon where the iron attachments are removed and the cement mortar from earlier restorations is cleaned off.

The Acropolis Committee plans to carry out a similar restoration programme for the Temple of Athena Nike. Until the year 2000 the Acropolis will continue to give the impression of a big work site crowded with scaffolding, machinery and workmen, presenting a picture surely similar to that of the Periclean period when this unique architectural ensemble was built. This way it will be possible to preserve these most splendid monuments of the ancient world for future generations, a heritage belonging not only to the Greeks but to the world.

DEMETRI PORPHYRIOS, CHEPSTOW VILLAS

THE RELEVANCE OF CLASSICAL ARCHITECTURE
Demetri Porphyrios

PROPYLAEA, ATHENS

In the last 25 years architects have articulated a devastating critique of the ideological assumptions of Modern architecture. The critique concerns both the aesthetics of architecture and the organisation of the city. For the Modernists, the ideal of reductive purity was ideologically charged and in this sense Modernist buildings were seen not only as things of beauty but also as anticipations of the radiant universal city of the future; in other

words, of a city that would stand as a symbol of a liberated and non-hierarchic society. In that sense, Modernism has been the only avant-garde movement of our century. This avant-garde commitment to such a goal of an emancipatory social liberation required, among other things, a refusal to look back to the various architectural traditions, all of which were supposed to have connotations of authoritarian domination. The old stylistic differences, whether regional, historical or attributable to class distinctions, were soon to dissolve. Style meant ornament, it meant decoration and since it symbolised status seeking, conspicuous consumption and display it was bound to be socially and morally objectionable, intellectually indefensible and aesthetically corrupt.

As regards urban design, we know that the Modernist approach was a radically rationalist *tabula rasa,* a clean slate: zoning, the city in the park, the free-standing building, the disappearance of the street, and the square, the destruction of the urban block. In short, it meant the destruction of the urban fabric of the city. All that was systematically hailed by the Modernists as an ingenious advance in urban social engineering. Take, for example, Hilbersheimer who claimed that 'every exception and every nuance must be cancelled out; abstract, mathematical order must reign so that it may constrain chaos to become form'. Hilbersheimer was neither the first nor the last Modernist planner. In the mid-19th century, Jules Borie had spoken of similar crystalline palaces for the brave new world and, I suppose, as late as 1969 designers like Superstudio still believed that their 'landscrapers' could be socially regenerative.

In my book on Alvar Aalto I have stressed this double objectivism of Modern architecture: the objectivism that aimed on the one hand at the mathematical abstraction of the city and on the other at the extinction of symbolic meaning. I discussed how Alvar Aalto emerged as a significant figure in the 50s and 60s exactly because he adopted strategies which appeared to undermine this double objectivism. In that sense, Aalto was the first modern eclectic and by extension the first Post-Modernist. In fact, Aalto had a catalytic effect in the debates which took place in the mid-60s between the Whites and Greys. Out of these debates two major concerns emerged: the importance of the rhetoric of style and the primacy of context. The whole Post-Modernist culture was indeed founded on these two concerns. Architectural thinking slowly moved away from Modernist planning towards contextual strategies and eventually towards a re-kindled interest in traditional urbanism.

The re-orientation which took place in the 60s and which later developed into Post-Modernism was and still remains based on an eclectic attitude. Much like 19th-century eclecticism, the aim of modern eclecticism has been to look at historical styles merely as communicative devices, as labels and clothing. Style itself was seen as having no natural relationship to the tectonics of building. Since this eclectic mood had nothing to do with the values of revivalism, it soon became clear that there could be no common criteria of aesthetic evaluation. Hence a pluralism that sprung out of 'an age of conciliatory culture, widespread, visiting the beliefs of all countries and all ages, accepting everything without fixing any part, since truth is everywhere in

L TO R : VAN PELT & THOMPSON, GENNADIUS LIBRARY, ATHENS; K F SCHINKEL, GLIENICKE PAVILION

bits and nowhere in its entirety'.

Many, including myself, have discussed the architecture of the last 25 years as historicism, contextualism, relativism or the aesthetics of accommodation. I don't want to take issue here with any of these interpretations. In a sense, all these accounts are accurate evaluations of our contemporary mood. If we are to understand, however, the phenomenon of Post-Modern architecture we must look at the distinctive use of its stylistic devices and conventions.

Modernism as an avant-garde made us familiar with the idea of showing rather than concealing the conventions and devices which are used in constructing a work of art. I refer here to what the Russian Formalists called the foregrounding of the device; an idea found in the alienation effect, for example, of Brecht. This idea of estrangement and foregrounding the device so character-istic of Modernism is maintained by Post-Modernism. Post-Modernist works show themselves for the contrivance they are, but in doing so they also state that everything else in life is a contrivance and that simply there is no escape from this. Hence the self-referential circularity of the Post-Modern quotation and the extreme fascination with parody and meta-linguistic com-mentary. Let me look now at the three major meta-linguistic idioms of Post-Modernism today: Post-Modern High-Tech, Post-Modern Classical and Post-Modern Deconstructionist.

The engineer's language of the 19th century had a direct relationship to the contingencies of construction and shelter. The social vision of the Polytechnicians gave it a futuristic aura which was to be exploited ever after by the so-called High-Tech architects. But as we know, Ferdinand Dutert's Palais des Machines was indeed a High-Tech building in the sense that it pushed the engineering skill of its time to its limits for a socially purposeful brief. On the contrary, contemporary so-called High-Tech buildings are only make-believe simulations of High-Tech imagery. It is in this sense that we can say that High-Tech acts today as a meta-language. The device, namely technologism, is shown here for the contrivance it is. In a culture where the frontiers of technology have moved away from building towards space and genetics, the idea of a High-Tech building can only be either wishful thinking or a make-believe.

The second idiom of Post-Modernism today is that of the Post-Modern Classical. Hansen's 19th-century Academy in Athens was a re-working of the Classical language where the principles of commodity, firmness, and delight were all respected. On the contrary, Post-Modern Classicists use the device of parody. They favour playful distortion, citation, deliberate anachronism, diminution, oxymoron, etc. Ultimately, this is yet another make-believe cardboard architecture.

Finally, Deconstruction today is marketed as a recent avant-

L TO R: TREASURY OF THE ATHENIANS, DELPHI; DEMETRI PORPHYRIOS, PROPYLION, VIRGINIA WATER

garde. But it is neither recent nor an avant-garde. It is but another version of the Post-Modern movement. The language adopted is that of the Constructivist avant-garde. But whereas the aesthetics of the Constructivist, say Chernikhov, were ultimately grounded in the social vision of an emancipated urban proletariat and in the hoped-for technology of the new industrial state, Post-Modern Deconstructionists today exploit the graphics of the avant-garde so that they may benefit by association and promote themselves as a new critical wave. They loudly reject such ideas as order, intelligibility and tradition. Architecture is supposed to become an experience of failure and crisis. And if crisis is not there, well then it must be created. In this respect, Post-Modern Deconstructivists lack a socially-grounded critical platform. If anything, Deconstruction today is a version of aestheticism. And let me add: those who claim amnesia have systematically resorted to historicism.

These three versions of the Post-Modern – Post-Modern High-Tech, Post-Modern Classical and Post-Modern Deconstruction – differ widely in their stylistic preferences, symbolic content and social constituencies but they share a similar scenographic view of architecture. This view of architecture as scenography can be summarised in Venturi's principle of the 'decorated shed': construction (firmness), shelter (commodity) and symbolism (delight) are distinct and unrelated concerns. They do not influence each other. Construction, shelter and symbolism are each governed by their own rules and they share no common aim. This scenographic attitude in the production of a building coupled with the fascination with parody I mentioned earlier are the two fundamental characteristics of the Post-Modern. Confronted with Post-Modern architecture one has a feeling somehow that all values have been researched and rejected. We are of this or that opinion just for the fun of it.

I have great respect for the inventive ingenuity of the Post-Modernists but I have repeatedly in the past criticised the Post-Modernists as regards exactly these two points: the principle of the 'decorated shed' and the aesthetics of parody. The self-paralysing parodies they thrive on, when unwrapped from their intellectualist idiom, are but dispirited commonplaces. If my view has been that of a Classicist, it has been so not because of a transcendental belief in the immutable nature of the orders but because I have come to realise that *Classicism is not a style.*

Let me clarify what I mean here. The critique launched by contemporary Classicists starts, quite significantly, not with the aesthetics of architecture but with the strategies of urban design. In other words, the critique addresses the destruction of the traditional urban fabric, the progressive abstraction of the city through zoning and the excremental experience of the Las Vegas Strip. The 20th-century city, argue the Classicists, works well

L TO R: C H HANSEN, ATHENS; T H JEFFERSON UNIV OF VIRGINIA

from the sewers up to the sky-scrapers as long as one considers the wastage in human and natural resources as a concommittant to the sustaining of the overall edifice.

Instead, the Classicists propose the wisdom of the traditional city: English, European, American or otherwise. The issue here is not one of stylistics but of ecological balance: to control the sprawl of our cities, to reconsider the scale and measure of the urban block, to emphasise the typological significance of design, to establish hierarchies between public and private realms, and to re-think the constitution of the open spaces of the city.

As regards the aesthetics of architecture, the Classicists adopt the theory of imitation. Art, it is argued, imitates the real world by turning selected significant aspects of it into mythical representations. Consider the following comparison. A documentary record of the atrocities of civil war can be contrasted with Goya's or Ruben's 'Atrocities of War' that depict Saturn devouring his children. The documentary record can only provoke disgust. Goya's imitative representation of the real world, however, does afford us aesthetic pleasure. This is so exactly because it establishes a distance from reality which allows us to contemplate our universal human predicament.

Similarly, a Classicist would argue, architecture is the imitative celebration of construction and shelter qualified by the myths and ideas of a given culture. Such myths might have to do with life, nature or the mode of production of a given society. Ultimately, architecture speaks of these myths and ideas but always through the language of construction and shelter. celebrating construction and shelter by means of tectonic order.

Surely, many Modernists have spoken about 'honest construction'. But I want to stress here that Classical imitation has nothing in common with the structural functionalism of Modern architecture. Modernism makes no distinction between building and architecture. Modernism does *not* imitate construction and shelter; it simply uses raw building material without any imitative mediation. In that sense, Modernism has produced buildings but, as yet, no architecture. The result has been a century of mute realism in the name of industrial production. On the contrary what makes Classical architecture possible is the dialogic relationship it establishes between the craft of building and the art of architecture. Our imagination traverses this dialogic space between, say, a pergola and a colonnade, and establishes hierarchies, levels of propriety and communicable systems of evaluation.

Classical architecture needs also another dialogic relationship: this time the relationship between one building and another. This point is very important. Today the market ethic of the original and authentic is based on the pretence that every work of art is an invention singular enough to be patented. As a consequence of this frame of mind, demonstrating the debt of, say, Giulio Romano to Bramante is today called scholarship but it would have been denounced as plagiarism were Giulio Romano still alive. I think it is unfortunate that it is not only the inexperienced Modern architect who looks for a residual originality as a hallmark of talent. Most of us today tend to think of an architect's real achievement as having nothing to do with the achievement present in what he borrows. Since we have been educated as Modernists we tend to think that our contribution comprises solely in that which is different. We therefore tend to concentrate on peripheral issues of stylistics.

What I am suggesting here is that the real contribution of an architect lies in what he/she chooses to borrow. Let us think for a moment of the greatness, say, of Alberti. His greatness lies in the fact that he gave a new life to the humanist theme itself which he passed on to the 15th century from the sources of antiquity. The world of Alberti was very different from that of antiquity; the technology was different, the politics were different, the *haute couture* had changed, but the great humanist theme of commodity – firmness – delight was still alive and will stay alive.

Let me finish by saying that architecture has nothing to do with 'novelty-mania' and intellectual sophistries. Architecture has nothing to do with transgression, boredom or parody. It has nothing to do with parasitic life, excremental culture or the cynical fascination with the bad luck of others. Architecture has to do with decisions that concern the good, the decent, the proper. Decisions about what Aristotle called the *EU ZEIV*, the good and proper life. Surely, what constitutes proper life varies from one historical period to another. But it is our responsibility to define it anew all the time. If we choose to embrace the tradition of the Classical we will find no recipes but we will encounter again and again a kind of genius for practical life, a kind of genius that is actually less of a gift than a constant task of adjustment to present contingencies. It is in this sense that we can speak of the Classical as that which endures; but this defiance of time is always experienced as a sort of historical present.

Versions of this paper were read at the 'Classicism' Symposium at the Tate Gallery, London, 1988, and at Neocon 21, Chicago, 1989.

ALLAN GREENBERG
Residence in Minnesota

ABOVE: FRONT ELEVATION; *BELOW:* SITE PLAN

This residence is set in the middle of forest land. The site for the house is a plateau at the head of a long valley. A lagoon in the valley is approximately a third of a mile long. It starts at the foot of the site and extends to a large lake. The area around the lagoon will be planted with daffodils and other bulbs

The design of the house is based on the play of symmetry set within the context of overall asymmetry. This reflects the condition of the site itself as the plateau is part of one side of the valley. The tall and massive roof, the major feature of the house, grows out of the dramatic contours of the site which rises high above it on two sides. On the entrance side, the house appears to be one-storey high with the two-storey entrance set back and cut into the mass of the house. Although the massing of the main house is symmetrical, the open service entrance and glazed conservatory on either side of the axis introduce an asymmetry which is further developed by the lower garage and bedroom wing extending out on one side.

The north elevation is quite different from the entrance facade. It is fully two-storeys high. The one-storey theme from the entrance is clearly visible as it comes around the west side of the house as an extended sunporch. This porch faces a waterfall on the opposite side of the valley. Glass is an important feature of the garden elevation taking advantage of the dramatic view down the lagoon to the lake. The living and dining rooms have projecting bay windows which are part of a continuous wall of glass running behind freestanding columns and entablature.

The house faces north. During the oppressively hot midwestern summers, the shaded terrace in front of the living, dining, family, and bedrooms is cool. In the harsh winter, the interior courtyard allows the sun to penetrate into the family room.

The house is built of unpainted redwood siding with cedar shingles on the roof. Columns and entablature on the north side, together with the two-storey entrance centrepiece on the south side is painted white. The retaining walls are of fieldstone. The two huge chimneys anchor the building to the site.

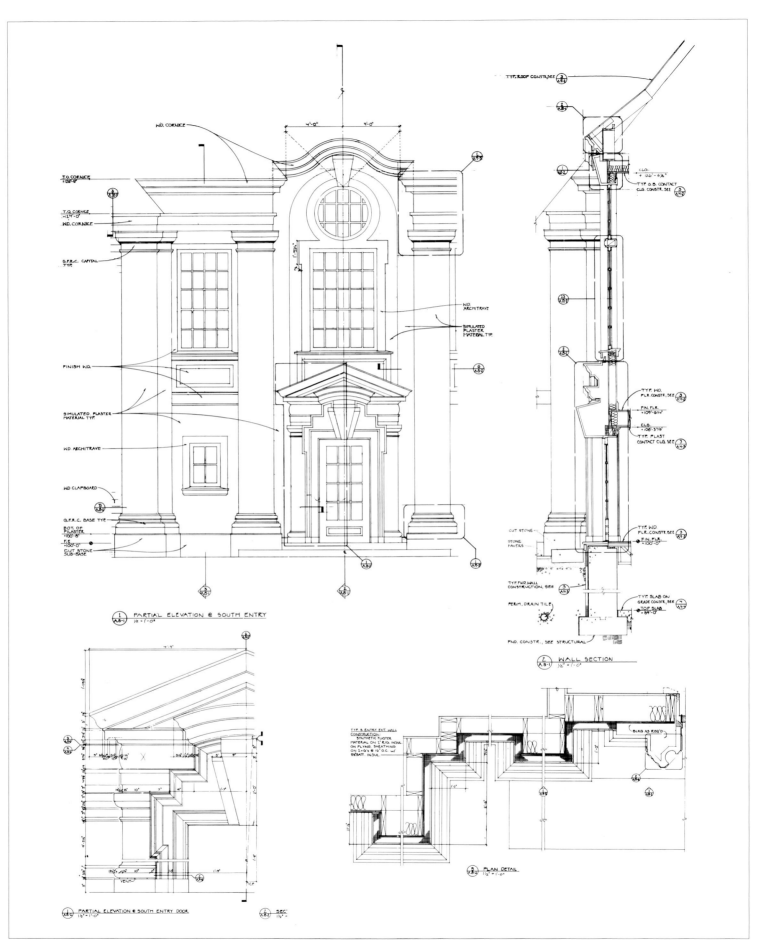

1 PARTIAL ELEVATION @ SOUTH ENTRY
A.8-1 1/2" = 1'-0"

2 WALL SECTION
A.8-1 1/2" = 1'-0"

3 PARTIAL ELEVATION @ SOUTH ENTRY DOOR
A.8-2 1/2" = 1'-0"

SEC.
1 1/2" =

PLAN DETAIL
1 1/2" = 1'-0"

WORKING DRAWINGS FOR FRONT FACADE

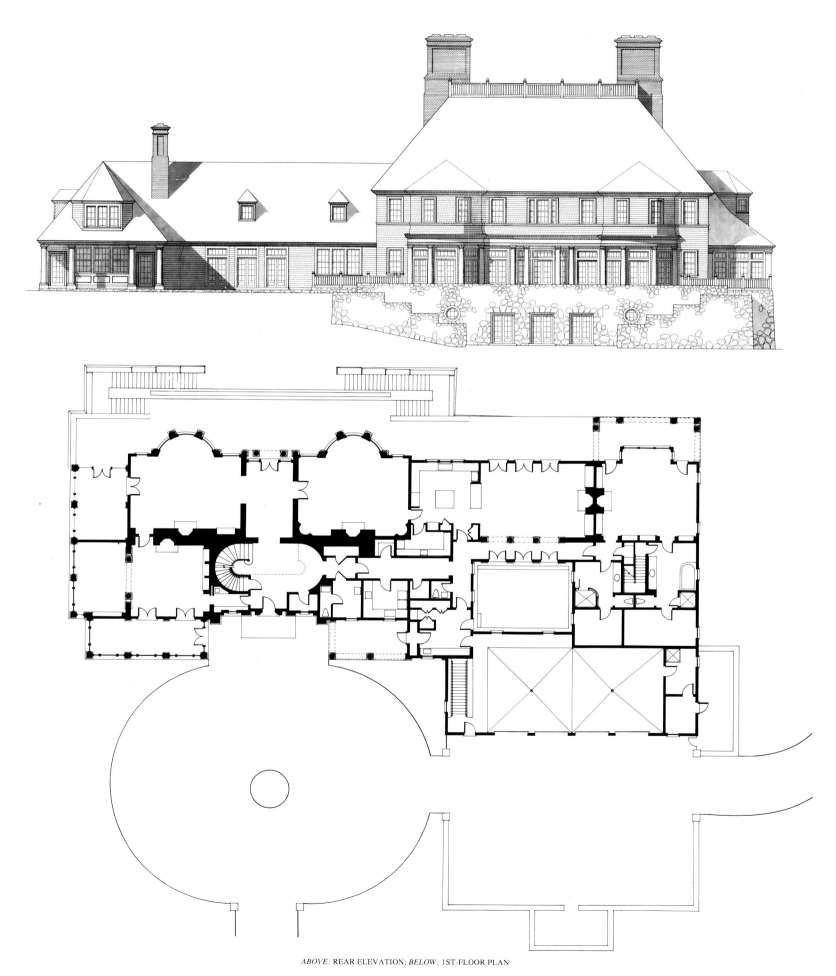

ABOVE: REAR ELEVATION; *BELOW:* 1ST-FLOOR PLAN

TRADITIONAL TOWNS
Andres Duany

SEASIDE AT DUSK

I have a depressing and aggressive analysis of what's happening in the suburbs. Aggressive because I assign blame, pointing out that the problems are due to this or that aspect of professional practice. The American town is a place of small buildings which are private houses and shops, and larger buildings that tend to be civic, like schools, churches, the city hall, and so forth. The little buildings are ordered along a mesh of small tree-lined ways

which are called streets. The civic buildings are attached to larger, rectangular spaces. These are called plazas or squares or greens, depending on the part of the country. All of these spaces look pleasantly habitable by people. There is individuality, the little houses and shops are each different, but there is also a great degree of agreement as to their relationship to the streets. An urban pattern which has existed from the eighteenth century until the 1950s – 200 years or more.

The city of Virginia Beach, a new American town, which is 'Becoming a showcase', is a place that only has large buildings. A place that has only one use. You see nothing but retail establishments, parking lots, and 10-lane roads. It is a town designed exclusively for the efficient movement of the automobile and its convenient parking. There are sidewalks, but no one has used them except indigents. These are the towns that we are planning now. They guarantee or attempt to guarantee the free flow of traffic, the sufficient provision of parking, and the absence of mixed uses. You shop here, and you live elsewhere, with buffers in between. Parking lots are always half empty, because they are rated now in our codes for the Saturday of Thanksgiving when the most Christmas shopping takes place. On this and 10 other days, the parking lots are full. The rest of the time parking lots are half empty. This is a well-planned town by the current standards. The only way that you can get around to do anything in towns like this is in a car. The car, in itself, is not a bad thing. The automobile is a great romantic instrument of liberation. But it is a completely hermetic, antisocial device. And worse, there is no choice but to use it.

The problem is not aesthetic, it is social. Each driver has a life structured on an eight-hour work day, plus two hours of discretionary time to be spent one between the place of living and the place of work in the morning, and another in the evening return. Those two hours, if they were not spent driving could be the most delightful, most constructive, most educational, most social, or most political of the day. If only a part of those hours could be spent walking and meeting our fellow citizens, or going to bookstores, going to cafes, meeting, discussing, reading, wandering. Those hours instead are spent aggressively competing for the limited amount of asphalt with their fellow citizens. Contact among fellow citizens is actually an aggressive, competitive, automotive contact under high stress for position on the highway and this is the only option that we have.

There is a horrifying statistic. If we work 243 days a year, which is what most Americans work, and if we commute one hour a day in the morning and one hour in the afternoon for each of the 243 days a year that the average American works, we would spend the equivalent of 60.75 working days in the car, or 12.15 working weeks! 12.15 working weeks spent unproductively, unpleasantly, and expensively, since we spend an average of $4500 per year on our cars. Now, take those 12 weeks that are not productive and add them on to the two-week vacation and make that a 14-week vacation and take the $4500 that you're sending to Hartford, Detroit and Tokyo, and spend it in Paris on your vacation. Now, that is something you could look forward to, except that those who would prefer to spend time in France with money in their pocket, don't have the choice of doing so because we are not building an urbanism where they can exercise this option.

What is being proposed here is not the irradication of the distant suburban house and the long drive for those who love their cars, but simply providing the alternative, a choice, which is not currently being implemented. Why is this so? Certainly not because the buyers don't want it. Marketing studies have concluded that Americans prefer to live in towns, and that they value community as much as security. In fact, those who want to live in towns are not being provided for because it is unlawful to build towns. Even if planners knew how to design towns, and even if developers wanted to build towns (neither of which is that difficult, it turns out), those developers would have to get variances from top to bottom, from street widths to mixed uses to the way cars are parked. Inadvertently, over the years, codes have been modified to the point that we can no longer build traditional American towns. We can no longer build Williamsburg, or Winter Park, or Nantucket, or Annapolis. We can no longer build the places that are among the great collective memories of America.

Miami in Kendall is an example of a contemporary planned suburb on the pattern of the 70s and 80s. It is by no means the worst I could find. The area is one of the square miles that the Continental Survey laid out in the 1790s. As such it represents a typical piece of America. Within it we find all the typical building and planning of contemporary America. There is a building complex surrounded by a sea of parking. It could be a shopping mall; some type of industrial park; it could be an office complex; or it could be a community college. As it happens, it is a community college, but it doesn't matter. For our purposes it can be any one of those massive new single-use complexes where hundreds of people work or shop. Next to, but disconnected from, is a welter of curvilinear streets with little houses along them. Zoning calls it R-5 (residential, five units to the acre), houses with little five-foot yards on the sides, and 20-foot yards in the front. It is also called the American Dream. Nearby, and again disconnected, are houses at two units to the acre, called R-2. These are for people exercising their option to particularly dislike their neighbours, or who particularly like to mow lawns. Presumably, they are wealthier sorts. There are town house clusters, also know as R-10, ten units to the acre and some R-16 zoning where are garden apartments three storeys tall.

At the highway intersection, according to the best current practice, are the shopping centres with their parking lots in front. You can also find churches, church schools, institutions or various types, post offices, and so forth. This square mile in fact has the right number of people living, the right institutions, the right amount of retail and workplaces. Current planning methods at their best do that. All of the ingredients of a community are being provided. Why then is it not a community, neither a neighbourhood, nor a town? This becomes clear when you analyse the daily experience of the people who live here.

Let us take as an example the professor who may live here. That professor, if he teaches at the community college nearby, could get there easily enough. It's well within walking distance. However, he can't there is a drainage ditch to bridge and then a huge parking lot. No 1980 vintage American will put up with that itinerary. It doesn't even occur to the person to walk. That professor instead gets in his car, goes out into the curvilinear street maze, down to the great collector street, enters the college parking lot, and parks at what turns out to be a couple hundred yards from his home. The same itinerary is forced on a person who lives close to the shopping centre. Or on a kid who goes to a church school nearby. The different parts of suburbia have been walled and separated. The planners have not provided internal connections from one place to the other. In fact, in some zoning

codes such connections are not permitted (you are not permitted to share parking lots).

The consequences are enormous. The first thing that happens is that every single event requires an automobile. The single family house in Florida, for example, is currently rated at 13 trips a day. The second is that every one of those trips uses the collector streets. That is why there is traffic congestion in even the very low densities of suburbia. There is enough roadway. The right amount of asphalt is always provided by the planners, but it is designed to lead all of the trips on to very, very few streets. This is why all the new suburbs from California to Florida have the densities of towns but the traffic of a metropolis. They have disadvantages of both types of urbanism: the culture of a rural town and the congestion of a metropolis. In New York or San Francisco, you put up with the congestion, but it's worth it, because there is plenty happening.

The result of all this, at a more personal nature, is that the hypothetical professor has to expend more of his salary than he really can afford to buy a second car, and if he has a teenage kid, a third car. That professor's savings go to Detroit for cars and Hartford for insurance. This personal tragedy particularly affects women. It assumes, of course, that mothers drive their kids around. That is not always the case, but it does happen, that many women are forced to drop their careers and become chauffeurs. In the suburbs, there is no place to live where the kids can be on their own to go to their classes, to visit their friends. They must be driven to visit their friends. If there are several kids, the trajectory is constant and complex. The only other option, and one frequently taken, is to affix the kids to the television set as surrogate entertainment. This is not without its harmful effects.

Because there is no incentive to walk, no one does, which is why suburbs have notorious reputations for being totally dead at night. In fact, some have very substantial population, but it is all indoors. There's no public realm, there's no street life, there's no social life. Everything in suburbia built since the 1960s suffers from that disconnection, and that disconnection often is legislated. What would it have harmed to connect that residential neighbourhood to these shops? Then the entire traffic load between them would have been exempted from loading that street.

In a traditional town, the radius of the curb should be no more than eight feet, because if it is eight feet, then the sidewalk can't approach it; and if there is, say, a 24-foot piece of asphalt, it is a leap of 24 feet to get across in this eight-foot radius. Now, if it's a 35- or 45-foot radius, that sidewalk can only approach to a certain point, and then the crossing gets doubled from 24 to 48 feet, which means that the amount of dangerous and unpleasant crossing has been doubled. Furthermore, buildings cannot get near to define exterior space. That is by code. We are constantly fighting this, and it is something that we are beginning to lose, because the Department of Transportation writes these rules, and the DOT and the God-like demeanor, because they are considered to be the only salvation against traffic congestion, will not grant exemptions. The first thing that has to happen is these curbs have to be able to be reduced to eight feet. That is decent and appears in all traditional towns, many of them with wonderful traffic patterns with semis and fIre trucks and garbage trucks and everything that you can imagine. The turning radii at Seaside are tiny; they're smaller probably than they should be, but certainly, we should not be forced with 45 foot radii.

There are many perfectly planned schools with statistically just the right capacity for the number of dwellings around, except that not one child in the history of these schools has arrived on his own. How would they get there? Who would permit them to cross these highways? Do you know what that means in terms of the life of the children here, that they cannot use the library when they want, or meet with their friends, or use the soccer field on weekends, or even stay after school socially, all because they have to be whisked away by buses and their parents' cars. They cannot decide when they want to go home.

If these same buildings were laid out differently first of all, some trips would be reduced by walking, so that each house would not generate 13 trips a day. And then most of those wouldn't load the collector street. Probably only three or four trips a day would emanate to the collector, which provides a substantial relief to the highway congestion. The building of new roads will do virtually nothing to relieve highway congestion unless it is accompanied by this type of planning. And besides, these connections would begin to establish a sense of community. Instead you have a shopping centre called the village corner store, except that there is no village and no corner, this shows that marketing wants these community ideas desperately. Marketing people know that wherever towns exist in good locations, they have high real estate value, higher than the new development. On-street parking is crucial to the existence of pedestrian life. And yet, planners everywhere are doing their best to strip parking from the roads and inadvertently are stripping life from our streets.

Traditional towns are terrifically resilient and terrifically able to sustain modern life and don't let any planners tell you that they don't work anymore. Just go there and see that they do work. In fact, what doesn't work are the modern suburbs that are congested. What ever happened to the civilised alleys that permitted the dumpsters and electrical transformers to be in the back? We have now become a society that is accustomed to step out of our front door and past the garbage dumpster. This would have been intolerable at any time until 1950. We have been forced to lower our standards. It is the duty of codes to encourage alleys and not to discourage them. They are as important as jogging tracks, if not more.

Another advantage of alleys is that they absorb the garages in small lots, which has a very beneficial effect on parking. If you have a small lot for townhouses or zero-lot line, the two garage doors are in the front and the front of the building facade becomes one of garage doors, and there is no way around it because cars can only approach from the front. Besides, the curb cuts the street from being used for guest parking. If alleys were implemented in urban plans, the garages would be in the back, the facades would be much more sociable, with windows and porches, and the entire street would be available for guest parking. Alleys should be in the ordinances and should not be considered a luxury. It is a most sophisticated way of resolving many problems of medium density housing. And one should add that kids love to play in these alleys. They don't play in playgrounds; they play in alleys. They want the hard surfaces for their balls and they want the toughness so they can bounce off and yell and make echoes.

Salem, North Carolina, is a pre-revolutionary town, a beautiful place. It has free-standing houses that Americans prefer. It shows that even the most delicate, old towns can absorb a modern complement of parking and traffic, and to make the point that cars, when parked on streets, look fine. It's incredibly unpleasant to be on a sidewalk and have a car go by, even slowly. It splashes; it makes noise and wind; it feels dangerous. When drivers see a street that is devoid of parking, they speed up. Drivers will go as fast as they think they can safely go, regardless of the speed limit, and it is usually too fast for pedestrian life. Only parked cars truly slow traffic, because drivers instinctively know that somebody might be pulling in or pulling out or opening a door, and they are cautious. They also protect the pedestrian. The pedestrian can wait between two cars, totally protected, and then make the crossing. Current planning manuals advise against it, because it slows up traffic, but that is precisely the need of a traditional street, as public space where both cars and people are comfortable. It is a balanced equation. There cannot be absolute ease of flow for the cars if, in fact, you are at the same time causing the unease of the pedestrian. It is the mix of the two that is important.

Another problem ensues if parked cars are removed from the streets: parking lots are created elsewhere. Streets have a tremendous ability to absorb parking loads in a graceful way. When cars are gone from streets, they don't look like parking lots, they look like nice streets. A parking lot is always a parking lot, and quite unpleasant, whether cars are there or not. There is a fundamental difference between a square or a street that has parked cars and a parking lot. The parking lot is always an antisocial space, a real estate negative. A view to a parking lot always lowers the real estate value, while a traditional street enhances the real estate value. People pay handsomely to live on the beautiful streets and squares of the world, although they contain both asphalt and cars. What is proposed instead is this. It is an enormous collector street. No parking is allowed on it because cars move along it. As a result, parking lots, these horrible places, have to be brought to the face of the houses. Why not put everything together, put the street, the parking, and the houses, and have enough budget left over to build alleys? The mentality of separation which separates residential from commercial and so forth has evidently now reached the point that different street types are now recommended instead of putting them all together in a single, coherent, traditional manner.

Haussmann would have welcomed some of the highways that we're building now. He would have seen them as fantastic real estate assets along which to build. The difference is that Americans have abandoned the highways to the car. Hausmann designed them as mixed use pieces. They contain every item that is required for a town. First, there are fast lanes, four of them, then there are two slow lanes, and then six parking lanes. The boulevards contain integrated parking lots; every 15 feet of length holds six parked cars. Mixed in are enough trees to form the equivalent of a park. It is not segregated. Also, there is high-income housing high in the buildings, middle-income housing lower, and low-income housing within the courtyards inside, plus offices and shops on the street. And it all adds up to such a charming place that right next to this twelve-lane highway, there is a fellow sitting at a cafe and enjoying it.

We are taking this national investment, these highly specified highways, and throwing them away because they are never put together like Paris. Central Paris, by the way, has 5,000,000 inhabitants, and it's a pleasure to live in. Suburban Miami has 300,000, and it is a nightmare to get around. Which planning is more efflcient? Is Paris archaic planning? Is this out of date, or is Kendall out of date?

The boulevard west of Boca Raton has the same number of lanes as the Parisian boulevard; it has comparable building uses; but instead of being a boulevard, it is a disaster. The best thing that can be said about it, is that it cannot even be remembered. You drive by one after another like this, and there's absolutely no memory of it. This is not the result of *laissez-faire*. This is not something that the developers wanted to happen. Every square inch of it, including the size of the bushes in the parking lots, was specified by the codes. Planners have the power to make architects and engineers and developers do exactly what they want. They are accustomed to being told what to do by the codes. It is just that what they are being told to do is this.

Now, the next issue is of some subtlety, and it shows the extent to which coding should perhaps play a part. California style has been the way Florida has housed itself throughout the 60s and 70s. As a design, it involves jogging units back and forth, back and forth. The more budget you have, the more jogs you get. One may say well, this is perfectly inoffensive; it is an easy composition; it gives individuality. Well, unfortunately, what happens is that street space in front is destroyed by the excess of articulation, because every bit of articulation prevents the making of a building wall, and spaces are made only when you have walls.

A comparable image is Georgetown. It is just a box with six windows and the same ingredients as before. There is asphalt, cars, landscaping, and building, but here the buildings are lined up, and so they make space, they make a public room, and when there is a room, there is life. The other one is a completely antisocial space, a parking lot that you flee because it is no place. This is the kind of thing that should be coded, that should not be let go. If the towns that emerge are to have a public life, one of the fundamental things is to make buildings line up in order to define public space.

One other element is important. The American street is too wide. They typical distance of building face to building face, relative to building height, exceeds the ratio of one to six, which is considered the minimum to define perceptible public space. It's too wide. The very best streets are no more than one to three; for example, Paris, which is wonderful, has a ratio of one and half to one; Florence, which is even more delightful, has a ratio of three to one. And yet trees in a steady row are an integral part of the American street, and make them the equal of any street in the world in beauty. Trees are not a dispensable ornament. It is a necessary part of the making of public space. And yet, our landscape architects rarely do this.

What the landscape architects currently designing suburbia do is create nice pictures for nice brochures. They act like decorators, but landscape is not a branch of decorating. It is a fundamental and integral part of defining public space, and it should be in the code that the landscape that many of the current codes require, should be used in a functional way to define street space. It is not just to make pretty; it is necessary to make social space. I have an entire collection of newspaper clippings having to do with the theme of being lost in the suburbs. The one about somebody who spent two days trying to deliver a package because they couldn't find their way in the suburbs. The streets are curvilinear mazes. There are planning manuals that encourage *cul-de-sacs*, the encourage curvilinear systems. One cannot find an address in a place like this. The stress of being lost is one of the primary memories of actually trying to make one's way here. These guardhouses exist not to keep crooks out, but to give instructions on how to find places. They're necessary.

Normally, curved streets are derived from topography. But planners use them for ornamental purposes even when the land is flat, as in Florida. What they're actually after is a terminated vista, which is to say that the view down the street should not go on forever. It is preferable to see the space closed in some way. Curvilinear streets will, in fact, guarantee a terminated vista, but only by happy accident. It is not actually designed and dependable. At best, this method results in a streetscape which is vaguely pleasant, but nothing that you can remember, somewhat like canned music, Muzak. There is nothing memorable, no landmarks, and that's why one is constantly lost in the new suburbs.

Coral Gables is a development from the 1920s with the highest real estate values in Miami. It is fundamentally a grid with exceptional diagonals, terminating vistas on public buildings so that you might avoid being lost, by periodically being able to see the public building which terminates many vistas. This requires controlled planning, in which roads are terminated by deflections. However, these intersections are no longer possible. Every one of the intersections in this book, which was a wonderful planning book, *Town Planning in Practice* by Raymond Unwin

of 1909, in this chapter on terminating vistas, is illegal by the current standards. Why? Because planners want the traffic to go through at all costs and they assume that drivers are unskilled and they would be unable to make turns like this one.

Our civic buildings should be located in special sites. Planners must preserve special sites for the schools, the post offices, the colleges, the fire stations, the police stations, that we build, and those locations should be more important than the usual location. Right now we locate schools on sites that could have been suitable for a supermarket. There isn't a hierarchy of sites that corresponds with a hierarchy of building. Charleston is one of the most memorable American towns. A place that brings tourists, not because it has a good climate or a good golf course or a good beach, but because it's a wonderful looking town, interesting to be in.

This is all very nice, but what about affordable housing? Now, that's a major issue. In desirable places like Cape Cod and Palm Beach County, all the real estate is very expensive. People who clean shirts and flip hamburgers and wait on tables cannot afford to live there. They're destined to enormous commutes to where the housing is affordable, and they're forced to own cars. In these places, planning departments are asking developers to build affordable housing as part of the permitting for more expensive housing projects. Developers fight it like the plague. They say that it will turn into a slum and that it will destroy real estate value all around. And they are correct. When you do put a substantial number of units of subsidised housing in one place it will destroy real estate value all around it, and you should not force developers to do that. But there are strategies that have worked well historically.

One can be seen in Annapolis, Maryland, and all over Virginia: a limited number of inexpensive, little houses, like these two 12-foot town houses, are interspersed with larger, more expensive houses. The necessary ratio of affordable housing to other housing is one in ten. If for every unit of one, you build ten of the other, then two of these affordable homes are surrounded by twenty of the others. As a result, the ratio of people with acceptable social behaviour will be able to overcome by example whatever nonelevated social behavior is presumed to emanate from the two small houses. Affordable housing is completely integrative if it is done in small clusters. You should never build more than six together. One in ten will solve the problem, so make every developer build one in ten, but not more than three in any spot. With more than that, there begins to form a little low-income neighbourhood, which will destroy real estate value.

Another strategy is also shown by an example from Annapolis. It is the apartment above the store. Now, it is said that people don't like to live above their store anymore and they may be right. Anybody who makes enough money to own a store, in fact, will probably not want to live above it. But that doesn't mean that a person who works at the store won't feel very privileged to live there. There is strong economic justification for this pattern: where land cost is high, developers cannot build affordable housing because the land cost when added to the construction cost will destroy the affordability. But if the store is actually scheduled to carry the real estate costs, the housing on top can be delivered at the cost of the construction alone. It doesn't have to carry the real estate cost. This pattern has the additional advantage that it is likely to remain affordable because it is a stigmatised place to live for many Americans.

The first pattern, unfortunately, will not remain affordable, because it is so nice that the first owners are going to reap a great profit when they sell and it will disappear from the stock of affordable housing. The apartment above the store, however, will remain affordable. All we have to do is zone that for every so many square feet of shopping centre, the developer must provide so many square feet of housing. That would solve the affordable housing problem for good. But as you know, mixed use is against most of Florida's codes, so it is illegal to address affordable housing in this manner.

The third strategy is also illegal in most places. It involves encouraging the outbuilding. There's a long tradition of these in America. Williamsburg is full of outbuildings. Small towns all over America have outbuildings. Coral Gables has outbuildings from the 20s. But not they're against the code. You cannot build a secondary dwelling, and it is policed by planning departments as if it were the plague coming into town. The reason is that it's presumed that if you build two units on each lot, you may overload the density and create a tenement in the suburbs. This is a genuine concern. The way to control it is to limit, by code, the number of square feet of the outbuilding unit to something like 400 square feet. At 400 square feet, an individual or a couple can live but not more people. So that's a simple way to control the negative effects of something that is otherwise socially beneficial. In fact, in England and Australia, you get tax breaks for building them. They're called granny flats. They solve the affordable housing problem. It keeps teenagers at home; it allows widowed parents to stay with the family without bothering the son or daughter-in-law excessively. And it allows people to rent. And there are other advantages to outbuildings. One is that the two hundred or four hundred dollars paid in rent supplement the income of the principal house holders which means they can afford mortgages earlier than they otherwise would. Another great advantage is that the rental premises are policed privately. Before renting, you can interview the prospective tenant carefully, because it's your backyard, making sure they're decent, making sure the stereo isn't on too loud, making sure they don't have excessively immoral practices. It doesn't occupy the local police department. It is the private policing of the low-income housing. Outbuildings alone, if allowed, would solve the affordable housing problem, but it is illegal.

Resistance to traditional developments does not come from developers. Marketing people have, evidently, arrived at the conclusion that a hometown is what people want. There was a national study done, asking retired people where they would prefer to live. 35 percent of them wanted to live in towns, 27 percent of them wanted to live in golf course communities, and then it went on down sharply to retirement communities. What they most wanted is not being provided.

California is ahead of Florida by 10, perhaps 20, years. We have no right to get things wrong because we can go to California and see what went wrong there already. And counties like Palm Beach County do not have the right to get it wrong when they can observe Dade County – the laboratory of failure is available at their doorstep. The current solutions to the traffic problem of Florida are two: one, you build highways, or two, you don't build anything. So we are building these highways at tremendous cost (spending as much on highways as on education, which is absurd).

But there's a third way, and California has just completed a study to this effect. The Southern California Association of Governments – a group of 30 municipalities around Los Angeles – recently completed a computer model of traffic patterns in the year 2010, in which they modelled all possibilities, including the double decking of the highways. The building of lanes all the way to the edge of the right-of-way, the subsidised expansion of the bus system, rapid transit. They modelled the mandatory staggering of work hours, and they modelled mixed use neighbourhoods. And their conclusion was that nothing that could feasibly be done would have anything but a cosmetic effect on the problem except for one thing, mixed use neighbourhoods. That would solve the problem.

At Seaside the highways do not work. Every dollar spent on a highway now is a dollar thrown away and best spent on education. A highway without purchase of a right-of-way and without bridges or anything, just a strip of six-lane highway is almost a million dollars a mile. Now, for that kind of money, municipalities can start buying pieces of real estate, demolish it, and complete neighborhoods to solve it permanently.

To build a highway is like having a heart bypass operation. Blood, or traffic, will flow for a while. But then it will plug up again. You also have to change the diet of the patient. You cannot bypass the heart and then keep eating cholesterol. You have to stop building these single-use places. There is no other chance, and there is no other solution.

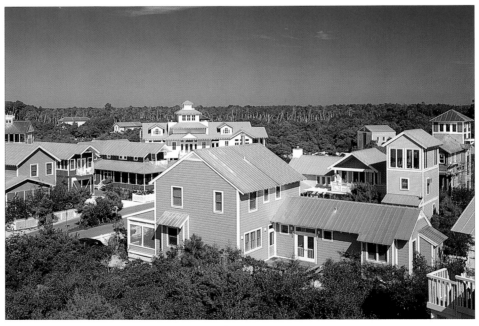

VIEW OF SEASIDE

THE THREE TRADITIONS OF MIAMI
Andres Duany

THE WOODEN VERNACULAR 'CRAKER' HOUSE

Miami is a young city, about 100 years since its settlement and less than 70 years in having even the most minimal urban presence. There hasn't been time to complicate matters and without doing violence to reality one can say that there are only three architectural traditions: The simple wooden vernacular of the first 40 years, called Cracker after the pioneers, the sophisticated and abused Mediterranean Revival of the 20's and that peculiar

brand of frivolous Modernism which began with the Brazilian in the 50's, passed through the hands of Morris Lapidus and is now spectacularly in the care of Arquitectonica. Each tradition emerged sequentially, but they did not entirely replace each other and they now coexist.

The thinking architects of Miami continue to work within one or another of these traditions and will defend the virtues of their preference as the only appropriate architecture for the place.

Each can make a strong case. The Cracker vernacular, for example, holds the high moral ground in every way. It has the honour of primacy since it was the shelter of first settlers. It is the virtue of being an austere architectural language derived from the straightforward expression of construction and materials. It is a light-weight wood architecture abundantly equipped with overhangs for rains and porches for breeze, and so the best fit for the hot humid climate.

Its proponents are generally the most self-righteous of Miami's architects. Here are two examples: the so-called 'Oldest House in Key West' which we restored in 1976 and our own essay of 1983, the Clary House.

This architecture is compelling to those rigorously educated architects of the 50's and 60's, but it is deficient in three ways which are important to the younger generation. The first is specific to the world of inexpensive speculative building which is Miami's primary industry, because it is too demanding in craftsmanship. Wood construction requires a degree of precision in the assemblage of the parts which drives the cost high relative to the forgiveness of stucco. The second is that it does not have

within its typological repertoire a sophisticated urbanism. Actually, individual porches can be aligned on streets, and the fences can successfully define public space, but when it comes to a real downtown, it can hardly deliver, and this is fatal to those architects for whom urbanism is the discipline of architecture. The third, and this is admittedly a self-indulgence, this architecture with so short a tradition cannot keep an academically inclined architect interested for a lifetime: A year or two of passionate study and then the great buildings are all known and there is nothing new.

The second tradition, the Mediterranean Revival, which followed in the 20's, more than compensates for this last deficiency. After all, it is the heir to the vast tradition of Antiquity and of the Rennaisance; of the anonymous towns of Italy, France, and Greece and also specific masters; Palladio, Schinkel, Wagner, Loos, Asplund and the young Aalto. It includes the High Game of Lutyens, which is enough for a lifetime of discovery and challenge.

Urbanistically, it is not necessary to extol the extraordinary quality and versatility of the Mediterraanean tradition. The architects of the 20's left us brilliant examples in Florida, perhaps better than the buildings. Furthermore, it is capable of sustaining not to say revelling, in mediocre workmanship. This is due to a historical circumstance which is uniquely North American: At the time that our architects discovered Spain and Latin America as a source, these places had been in economic decline for centuries so the Mediterranean 'style' was brought home, with a component of romantic decrepitude which has proven very well adapted to our impoverished building culture. This is why all the inexpensive buildings of Miami are in some measure Mediterranean.

Climatically, the masonry buildings with thick walls and small openings might not be the best for natural ventilation, but they are superb for air conditioning which is, in any case, the real climate of Miami now. If some continue to have the archaic habit of enjoying the fresh air, certain elements of mediterranean architecture like the loggia, the courtyard, and the tower, they would not do without.

The bulk of our work has been within this tradition; sometimes pretending to play the High Game like at the Atrio House, sometimes bypassing the local influence and exploring the roots like the Greek Villanova House or the Roman De La Cruz House. All have been learning experiences and presumably they have not only prolonged and enriched the tradition in Miami, but also cleansed it. In Miami an undisciplined Post-Modernism is commonly grafted onto the Mediterranean tradition causing great damage to its reputation. A recall to order seems to be necessary.

The Mediterraneans are viewed as hopelessly degenerate and self-indulgent by the Calvinist Crackers and hopelessly timid and retardataire by the glamorous Modernists. And yet any architect who has worked within this sophisticated tradition cannot possibly simulate the charming ignorance of the Crackers nor the militant amnesia of the Modernists.

The third tradition, the Miami Vice Modernist, also manages to hold a portion of the high moral ground. This miraculous achievement, is possible only in the current intellectual climate. Its urbanism achieves magnificent images from the moving automobile and then the convenient storage thereof. The public places, when they exist, are only the private lobbies of condos and the malls of shopping centers. Yet the Modernists monopolize the holy prerogatives of creativity and the spirit of the time. While one may know better, there is something solid about the tradition of Miami Modernism, otherwise this architecture would not be so compelling.

The modernist arguments are strong. It is an architecture that appears to be indigenous to Miami. It isn't, of course, but the real spawning grounds in post-revolution Moscow and the playgrounds of Brazil, could never have sufficient wealth to execute the spectacular frivolities of this brand of modernism. k is now, with the help of Miami Vice the export image of Miami. The reality is that of a hard-working, productive city of immigrants but that is not a glamorous product.

Perhaps because of its genesis via Latin America, this tradition has none of the sanctimonious, socially conscious, constructionally honest, restraints which so dulls modemism in the eyes of the public. Unhampered, it is fantastic and radical and a much- needed leavening for the other two traditions which are conservative through and through. The masters of the Cracker and the Mediterranean have no instinct for the astonishing, only for the amusing, no teste for the radical, only for the correct.

The three architectures of Miami have their strengths and that is why there are no converts. The architects debate and argue but no one of consequence has gone over to another side.

We have become convinced that a truly regional architecture must include the strengths of all three and have undertaken, in our latest work, the challenge of a comprehensive synthesis.

In this endeavor, we have found that the synthesis of any two is not great feat. The Mediterranean and the Modernist are natural complements as everyone since Asplund and Irving Gill has known. We have sometimes varied the proportion of the genetic pool, like the Prado House and the Hibiscus House, but we have not always avoided monsters; like The Williams Apartments or the Galen Offices.

The Mediterranean and the Cracker also breed beautifully and generate fine civilized offspring, after all they are both from good families. The work in St. Croix is of this derivation.

The difficulty in architecture, as in human reproduction is the breeding of all three seemlessly, without creating monsters of eclecticism. With two new houses, we have the beast. The Rosen and Socol Houses combine the sober massing and sophisticated columnar discipline of the Great Mediterranean Villas; the crispness which articulates the wooden cracker houses and the spatial excitement and dimensional extravagance of the modernist buildings. At least we hope so.

The Rosen House has an entrance through which both the car and the pedestrian enter in the best Modernist manner, to be rewarded by a Mediterranean atrium complete with impluvium. The Socol House makes use of the Mediterranean podium which holds lightweight Cracker porch and a breezeway within called a 'dogtrot' that both are of exaggerated Modernist proportion. Within both of the houses, within the discipline of roof and columns, there sits a free plan which, if not quite of Modemist abandon, is certainly more open than is normative within the other traditions. The Socol House uses precast concrete telephone poles which approximate the proportions of slim wood construction while the Rosen House experiments with the more stately proportion of the Royal Palm. There is a tradition in the Cracker vemacular of using palm trunks in this way. Could this be the Miami order?

We await the result of this gene-splicing without anxiety; for better or worse, the tropical landscape will swallow both.

L TO R: THE MIAMI VICE MODERNISM OF WILLIAM APARTMENTS; CORAL GABLES, MEDITERRANEN REVIVAL

DUANY & PLATER-ZYBERK
Three Projects

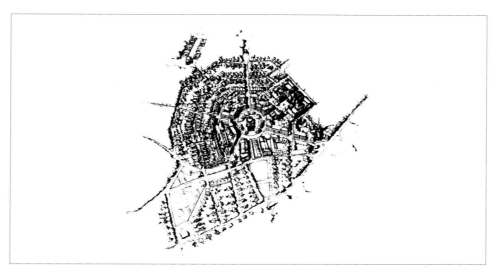

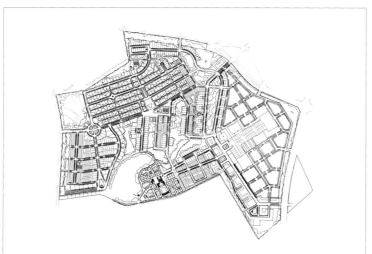

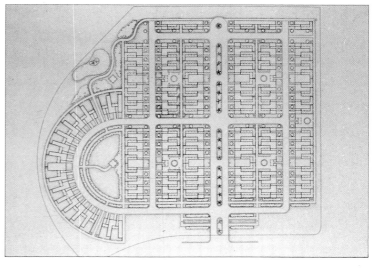

Above: Aerial view of the village of Crab Creek showing clearly the axes and centre on which it is planned; *Centre L to R*: Plan of Kentlands, Gaithersburg, Maryland showing the different sets of grid formations; perspective of a street in Kentlands showing house styles. *Below L to R*: Photograph of a street in Charleston Place with colour giving each house its individuality; overall plan of Charleston Place illustrating the distinctive layout.

VIEW FROM THE STREET

CHEPSTOW VILLAS, LONDON, 1988
Demetri Porphyrios

VIEW FROM THE STREET

This is a new building in the residential area of Holland Park. A 50's structure had replaced the mid 19th-century urban villa which was destroyed in the war. This Modern concrete building was a rather unfortunate intrusion into the otherwise undisturbed urban fabric of the street and we took the view that it should be demolished.

The street has a well-defined type of spacious detached villa which is finished in render and features prominent entry stairs and porticoes on rusticated bases. Though detached, the houses are very close to each other so that their front elevations are emphasised while their flank walls are treated in a circumstantial and contingent manner.

Early in the design we decided to maintain the existing urban and iconographic rules of the street. This meant maintaining

VIEW OF CONSERVATORY

the tripartite organisation of the facade, both vertically and horizontally. But whereas originally these were single family houses, our brief asked for an urban villa comprising two maisonettes, four one & two bedroom apartments and a penthouse. The design challenge, therefore, was to devise a scheme that respected the urban hierarchies of the street while providing accommodation of a repetitive nature.

On the front elevation we maintained the tripartite organisation horizontally but only the two bays have windows. The central bay is a soaring void which becomes itself a portico that is roofed by the broken pediment. This broken pediment and the pedimented entry door have a sculptural quality which is contrasted to the unadorned surface that separates them.

The garden elevation is a simple wall

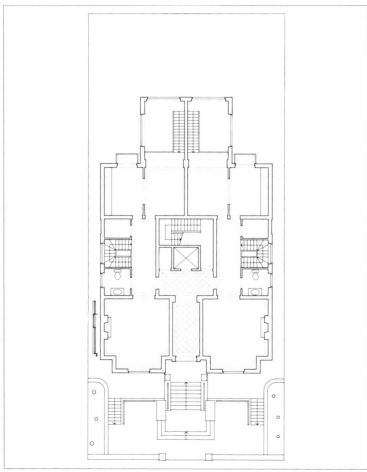

ABOVE: PENTHOUSE DRAWING ROOM; *BELOW L TO R*: GROUND FLOOR PLAN; ENTRANCE LOBBY

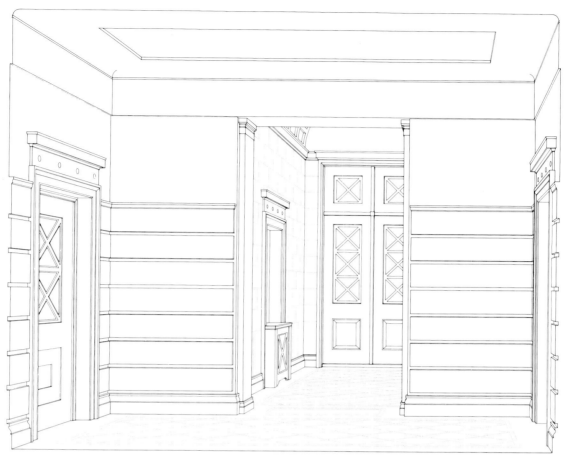

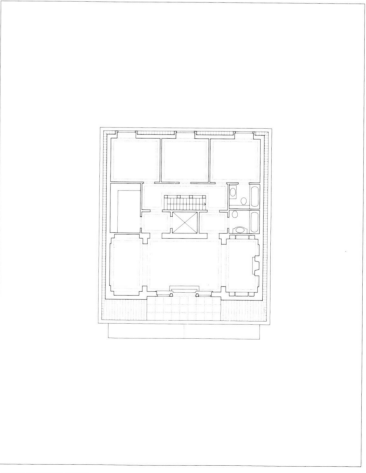

ABOVE: ENTRANCE LOBBY; *BELOW L TO R*: ENTRANCE LOBBY; TYPICAL FIRST AND SECOND FLOOR PLAN

GARDEN ELEVATION

pierced by windows. It is here that the repetitive nature of the brief is revealed. A separate skylit volume is appended onto the building in an additive manner and it houses the two conservatories of the maisonettes. The projecting timber eaves and perimeter trusses give the conservatory an appropriate rustic quality without, however, compromising its reading as a 'machine in the garden' which derives from its scale and tectonic rationality.

The plan is organised front to back and around a central lift and service staircase. At ground level the public lobby is one and a half storeys high and at each floor there are smaller lobbies that give access to the left and right-hand side units. At penthouse level the rooms are organised around an occupied centre; an inversion of the cortile-type plan.

This is a masonry wall building on a raft foundation and with concrete floor flat slabs. Externally the whole is rendered and painted in off-white except for the timber members of the conservatory which are painted in olive-green. The front steps are in Yorkstone and all profiles to cornices, pediments, architraves, coronas, sills, diestones and rusticated base are formed *in situ* in render.

Internally walls are plastered and painted. The entrance lobby has marble floor, incised and/or rusticated walls and a coffered barrel-vaulted ceiling. All internal cornices, coffers and anthemia have specially made profiles in fibrous plaster. We have also designed the light fittings for the entrance lobby, all metalwork for railings as well as all architectural joinery, including wardrobes, radiator casings, skirtings, architraves, doors and windows.

DESIGN TEAM
D. Porphyrios
A. Sagharchi
I. Fleetwood
M. Bradbury
I. Sutherland
R. M. C. Wilson

STRUCTURAL ENGINEERS
Trigram Partnership

CLIENT
Balli development Ltd

CONSERVATORY

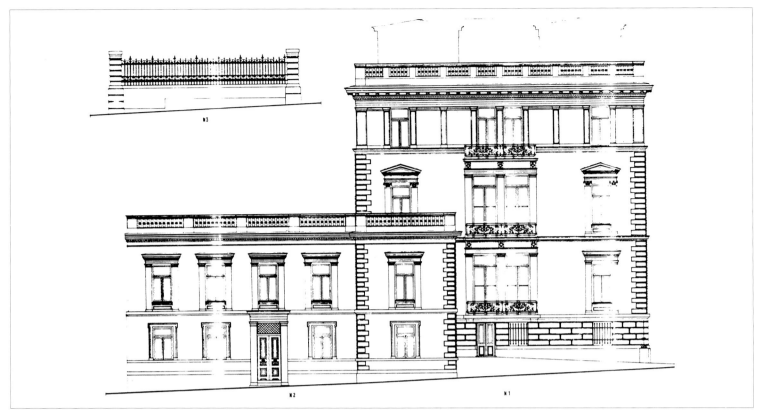

ABOVE: SOUTH FACADE, RESTORATION DRAWING; *BELOW L TO R:* DETAIL, AFTER RESTORATION; SOUTH FACADE, AFTER RESTORATION

C P MYLONAS
Restoration of
the German Archeological Institute in Athens

ORIGINAL BUILDING IN 1900

The Annex of the German Archeological Institute in Athens was financed by famous archeologist Heinrich Schliemann and designed by well known German architect Ernst Ziller living in Athens. Later additions were designed by architect and archeologist Wilhelm Doerpfield, then director of the Institute. The restoration works were concentrated on the repair of the facades of the whole complex and the rehabilitation to its original form and context. Original materials and techniques were used and lost features were restored. Where necessary, improvements were achieved with the use of modern materials and technology. Replacement elements were copied from the original.

Where possible, stucco-mouldings were retained, being bright samples of highly skilled 19th-century workmanship. Rustic quoin imitations were reconstructed in the traditional way, while carpentry was replaced and balustrades reconstructed. All facade wall-surfaces were smoothed with a trowel, pressed over and over again, until a perfectly even surface, almost polished was achieved. External surfaces were coloured by spraying in two to three very fine layers, thus avoiding brush marks and reducing the risk of peeling. It also achieves a texture very close to the original lime-washes.

Correct colouring was one of the major concerns, and was determined through microstereoscopic examination of original colour and through archive research. All elements imitating marble structures were coloured in five different shades of *blanc-casse*, while the extensive main wall-surfaces were painted in a light ochre-yellow colour, and the background of the decoration surfaces at the top floor in a brick-red shade, with almond-green frames. A slightly faded grey green colour was used for wooden parts, like shutters. Thus, though sober and restrained, the building remains colourful and light.

The project was carried out by the architectural firm of CP Mylonas in Athens, and was awarded a *Europa Nostra* diploma of merit.

OCTAGONAL LIBRARY, CENTRAL COURT

CHARLES SHOUP
House near Koroni, Greece

GARDEN GROTTO

Richard Economakis and Michael Lykoudis

Charles Shoup is an American architect and painter who has been active in Greece for some 30 years. Among his creations is this remarkable villa near the little town of Koroni in the southern Peloponnese, which is now in the process of being completed. It sits by the sea against a rugged landscape of grey limestone rocks and cypress trees, commanding views of the Messenian Bay and distant peaks of Mt Taygetos. With its handsome gabled masses it breathes new life into the country's Classical tradition and reaffirms historical notions of space and enclosure.

The house draws inspiration from works of the Romantic movement and the so-called 'Danish School' which was active in Greece during the first half of the 19th century. Its carefully articulated facades capture the rustic elegance of Theophilos Hansen's residential work in post-revolutionary Athens, making references to the architecture of Classical Greece and emphasising 'archaeologically correct' forms. At the same time the informal nature of the plan with its tree-filled courts and gardens and casual display of antique fragments recalls Schinkel's picturesque compositions at Schloss Charlottenhof and Gleinicke. A generous use of ornament and decorative elements heightens the aesthetic qualities of the building providing symbolic richness. Within its framework of Hellenic revivalism the house expresses unusual inventiveness and originality and stands out as one of the most exceptional examples of contemporary Classical architecture.

The plan is arranged around a U-shaped court which opens onto a series of terraced gardens and patios. It is entered through an elegant portico and smaller court to the west, opposite a curved stair that forms part of a long entrance axis. A fountain in the central court acts as a focal point for this axis, and intersects another that links the building to the gardens. These two alignments are the principle organisers of the house and are formally differentiated by their respective use of the Doric and Ionic orders. Living room, bedrooms, and kitchen occupy corners of the court and look out over the landscape. The Dining room is expressed as an octagonal tower, a reference to the Tower of the Winds in the Athenian agora, with clerestory windows at the end of the garden axis. Directly across the entrance to the court, a second arched portico is connected by a stair to a lower level of guest rooms.

In section the building adjusts itself to the sloping topography while expressing

EAST ELEVATION (FACING BEACH AND KORONI)

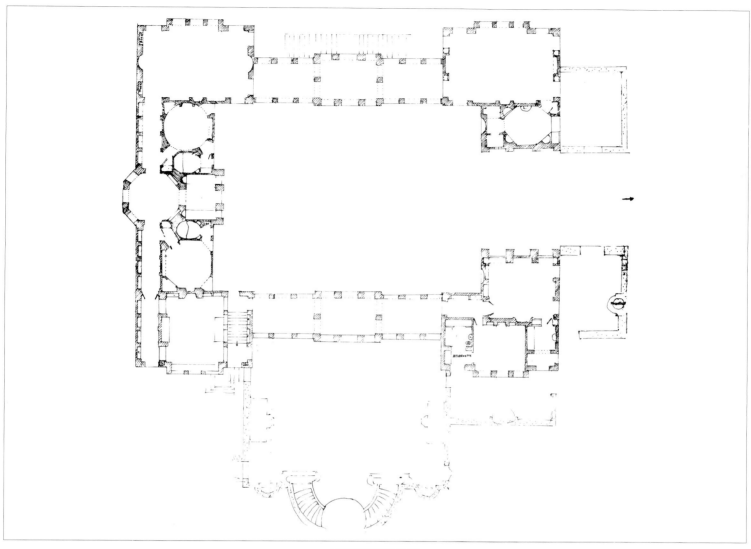

GROUND FLOOR PLAN

the orthagonal nature of the plan. Stepped terraces allow the grounds to spill into the more enclosed courts and gardens, and help to define the spaces. The entrance axis carries across the descending levels, which act as stops in the approach and provide views of the surrounding landscape.

When Shoup began to build here a little more than a decade ago, the site was a barren, inaccessible slope with no standing structures except for a few old retaining walls. After terracing and levelling the grounds he laid the foundations of a rough plan which he continued to refine during the process of construction. Except where natural materials were meant to be expressed, the building employs a structural system of massive stone walls on the lower level upholding brick construction above. In keeping with the local vernacu-

lar style, walls are stuccoed and painted a light ochre with white trim, and exterior cornices are made of wood. To enhance the rustic qualities of the house, conspicuous use is made of older, weathered materials. Many of the roof tiles were rescued from dilapidated houses in the area, and terracotta capitals and acroteria selected from dusty collections in architectural antique shops. Discarded bricks from old houses in Athens are applied in a variety of interesting ways, principally Byzantine, along eaves and cornices, around doorways, and as parapet rails.

Use of the orders is confined to the Doric and Ionic, which Shoup feels are most appropriate given their origins in the architecture of Classical Greece. Doric pilasters articulate the porticos that face the central court along the entrance axis, and line the walls of two small galleries

that lead into the Dining room tower. The Ionic order appears on the facade and interior of the Dining room, where freestanding wooden columns that were salvaged from an old British merchant vessel flank pedimented doorways. A large portal on the tower's north elevation is framed by rows of rosettes, as in the north porch of the Erechtheion.

One of the most impressive aspects of the building is its spirited use of architectural ornament. Winged griffins and elaborate antefixae, sculpted by the architect, grace pediments, and marble reliefs surround niches and recessed alcoves. Large garlands adorn panels above the entrances to the central court and reappear on the rusticated walls of a garden grotto. On either side of the two Doric porticos, life-sized statues of mythological gods look out over the rooftops. Sculpture occurs

79

ABOVE L TO R: EAST FACADE WITH STAIRWAY; LIBRARY, NORTH ENTRANCE ; *BELOW L TO R*: WEST ELEVATION DETAIL;VIEW PAST ENTRANCE COURT TO CENTRAL COURT

VIEW OF HOUSE FROM MESSENIAN BAY

less formally throughout the grounds, whether at the ends of axes, along garden paths, or in isolated locations. Caryatid herms form a circle around the fountain in the main court and support a grapevine trellis that ties into the walls of the house. The informally arranged fragments that are displayed against the architectural background act as historical footnotes to the building's stylistic themes, and recall the exhibits in John Soane's Museum in Lincoln's Inn Fields. Occasional Islamic motifs and inscriptions make reference to Greece's years of Turkish rule, and a charming Turkish garden with a brightly coloured patio and towerlike dovecote hugs the north side of the house.

The terraced gardens are an integral part of the design and are axially organised on either side of a paved walkway that leads out of the central court. Sculptural

elements and picturesque ruins are used to mark specific locations and relate thematically to the rest of the site. Large, decorative gates that connect the terraces are treated as vignettes that combine the building's various architectural and aesthetic features. A paved patio with elegant geometric patterns provides splendid views across the water to Koroni. At the end of the garden axis a statue of the earth goddess Demeter looks out from the darkness of a grotto, which makes use of diminishing perspective and alternating layers of rusticated walls to heighten the perception of depth. Just inside the grotto, a small circular basin connects back to a rectangular pool by means of a narrow channel, symbolically linking the divinity and her powers of fertility to the grounds.

Shoup did not set out to build this house as a means by which to display his

thoughts on architecture or as a polemic in favour of Classicism. He quietly busied himself over the years with the creation of an environment that satisfies his own desires and expectations. Here his love for the past and artistic sensibilities have come together in a unified composition that is contemporary in its essence, yet full of romantic nostalgia. The scattered architectural fragments that have been incorporated into the house are not so much the ruins of buildings that are gone but rather the foundations of a rich tradition on which he has built.

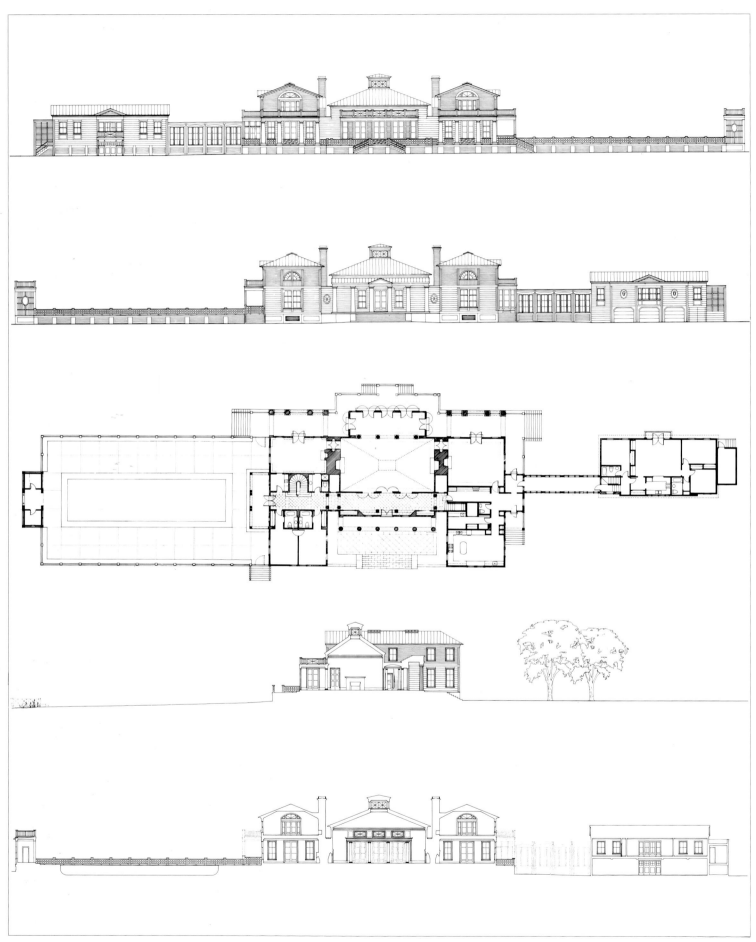

FROM TOP TO BOTTOM: WEST ELEVATION; EAST ELEVATION; PIANO NOBILE PLAN; CROSS SECTION; LONGITUDINAL SECTION

COOPER, ROBERTSON AND PARTNERS
Ertegun Villa, Eastern Long Island

VIEW OF MODEL

The programme comprised a symmetrical arrangement of rooms in the Neo-Classical tradition, opening onto porches and terraces overlooking the water: Library, Salon, Winter Garden, Dining Room on the ground floor with Master Bedroom, Guest Rooms and service spaces arranged around these on two floors. The main building was to be connected both to a swimming pool and to a garage and caretaker's house.

The site consisted of five acres overlooking, to the west, an estuary of Shinnecock Bay and bordered on the other three sides by a luxurious residential precinct. The land is virtually flat, with a number of trees on its upland side, and marshy wetlands with shrub growth bordering the shoreline. The complex is, accordingly, raised on a plinth affording sweeping views over the marshes and water.

The siting strategy grew naturally out of the programme, the requirements of view and access, environmental constraints and formal precedents. The house, approximately 10,000 sq ft, occupies a 75 ft wide band running north/south across the middle of the site, dividing the wetland from the upland lawns. Formal access is from the east on a curving gravel drive, which leads into a square forecourt; service access is from the north. The site is bounded on three sides by privet hedges and an apple orchard occupies the northern end of the wide lawn with kitchen gardens on either end of the garage.

The plan, symmetrical and U-shaped, is composed of a single high-ceilinged Salon with flanking two-storey 'wings'. A long gallery ,connects these three elements and extends the north/south site axis through the house and out over the pool deck.

Raised above the entry court is a stone terrace and shallow porch with large-scale Doric columns. This opens into the front hall gallery which reveals the cross axial arrangement of the plan. The three front rooms open onto covered porches (Tuscan) and an enclosed Winter Garden (Ionic). Light is admitted through high, triple-hung windows, French doors, lanterns and skylights. The rooms are high ceilinged and simply detailed.

The entire house is sheathed in varying widths of horizontal (cedar) siding painted a rich saffron colour, with white sash, doors and trim; corners and wall-openings are framed in vertical boarding. The roof is raised-seam copper. Interior finishes include stone and wood floors, plaster and panelled walls and painted wood trim.

The house, now under construction, is scheduled for completion in Spring 1990.

ABOVE: SOUTHEAST ELEVATION; *CENTRE*: SOUTHWEST ELEVATION; *BELOW*: SITE PLAN

VIEW OF WEST FACADE

Private Residence

East Hampton, one of the most beautiful villages in the north-east, carries implicit and subtle instructions to those who intend to build and live there. Layered over now with 'country chic', the village still retains the emotive power of a Yankee tribal place, so that even among the collection of succeeding resort styles there is a constant reminder of sterner times, of the inherited habits of weather, landscape, materials, occupations, and origins.

This private residence attempts to combine aspects and activities of the earlier rustic cottage with those of the more formal estate, within a rectangular and self-contained world which provides for entertainment, privacy, service, sport, and gardening. Trees, paths, fences, flower beds, surrounding hedges, a pool and carriage house are the permanent elements of this site; the fixed dock, one might say, to

which the house is moored.

The cottage employs a number of traditional local devices: an expansive porch onto which major rooms, laid out as a series of bay windows, open; an emblematic large window facing the main street; 'Dutch' gable roof asymmetrically shaped so as to delineate the south 'front' from north 'back'; small-paned dormers; screened service courts; and a richly-shingled exterior. In this sense, the house is 'traditional'. Its ground-floor plan, however, is unlike that of its older neighbours, shaped to a more informal style of living, with discreet smaller rooms supporting the continuous, open living areas (breakfast room, dining/library, living room) and a deep wrap-around porch which serves as a summer living room — the real and symbolic 'core' of the house. A central, 'colonial' hall, perpendicular to

the porch, skewers this enfilade of front rooms, taking the long axis of the site through the house. Whereas the south front is high-roofed, symmetrical and formal – of a scale to hold the expanse of the private lawn – and is centred by a large open dormer which marks the hall/entry axis and entry, the north and more public side is low-eaved and asymmetrical, expressive of the various interior service areas and related to the smaller kitchen garden behind the house. This is a reversal of the usual American 'formal/front, informal/back' arrangement vis-à-vis the street, but one with local precedent. The narrow and end elevation becomes the primary face of the house . . . a reaffirmed quintessential regional silhouette.

The house was sited to optimise natural light and nestles around several specimen trees.

HAMMOND BEEBY AND BABKA
The Harold Washington Library Center, Chicago

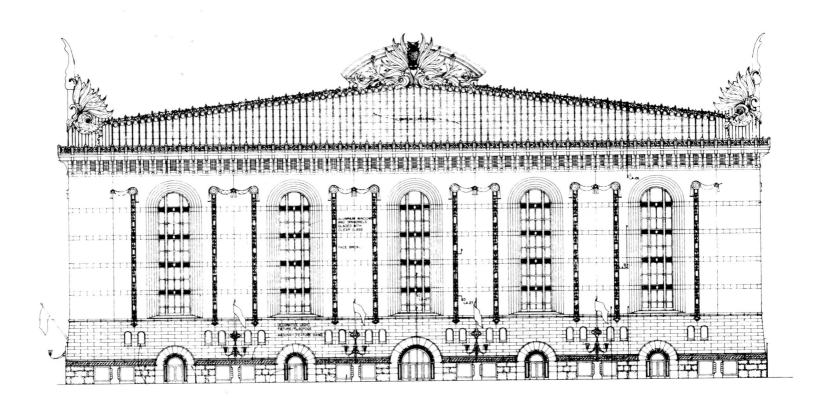

EAST ELEVATION

The Harold Washington Library Center is to serve as the central library for the City of Chicago. The ten-storey, 70,000 sq ft building is to be built on a site bounded by State Street, Congress Parkway, Van Buren Street and Plymouth Court.

The design intends to inform the user of its role as a public building within the City. The use of ornamentation fulfills its traditional role of breaking down the scale of the building to human dimensions while sustaining the degree of monumentality appropriate for a civic structure.

The exterior is intended to respond to its context on both a cultural and physical level. The base is rusticated and composed of monumental granite blocks. The brick wall above is broken by recessed arched openings that gather the windows of many floors into one large and recessed aperture of monumental scale. The projecting cor-

VIEW OF MODEL

nice at the top of the brick facade completes the Classical breakdown of the building into base shaft and cornice.

The interior organisation is a result of the need for a flexible, typical library floor plan that would still allow for a sense of spatial definition. The solution begins with the fact that a building is fixed at its perimeter as well as its top and base, and that the central block offers the greatest opportunity for flexibility.

The aim of the design was thus to provide a functional library building combining a maximum potential for flexibility with a sense of spatial definition and an architectural expression appropriate for a civic structure in Chicago. The building will be completed in 1991.

Design Architects: Hammond Beeby and Babka, Inc; *Project Architects*: Dennis E Rupert, Charles G Young.

86

SCULPTURE COURT

The Daniel & Ada Rice Building, The Art Institute of Chicago

The Daniel F and Ada L Rice Building is the latest addition to The Art Institute of Chicago, which exhibits varied collections of art. Since the construction of the original 1893 building, numerous additions and remodelings have expanded the Institute's capacity within a prescribed site. The new wing is organised about a major cross axis extending the planning principle of the original building. The existing conditions of the site included two small one-storey buildings, which were demolished, and a major portion of the existing plant facilities which were upgraded and incorporated into the three-storey addition. The lower level consists of gallery space for European Decorative Arts, Textile Storage, staging space for Special Exhibitions, shops and mechanical service space. The second level consists of a two-level skylit sculpture court,

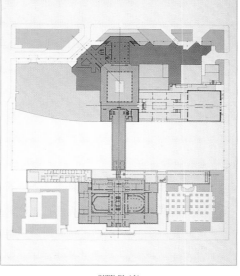

SITE PLAN

gallery space for the American Arts Collection, art storage for American Art and European Decorative Arts, and art handling and shipping space. The third level consists of skylit gallery spaces surrounding a balcony overlooking the sculpture court, a 16,000 Sq ft special exhibitions gallery, audio/video rooms, store, and a loading area for shipping and receiving of artwork.

Without infringing the existing exhibitions space, the Daniel F and Ada L Rice Building increases the Institute's gallery area by 33% and provides a large permanent space to hold special exhibitions and the necessary areas required for the auxiliary support functions for majoring travelling exhibits and new permanent galleries.

Design Architects Hammond Beeby & Babka, Inc; *Project Architect*: Dennis E Rupert.

THE CITY AND CLASSICAL TRADITION
Manuel Iñiguez

The redevelopment of Chateau Pichon-Longueville at Pauillac, Bordeaux, France by M Iniguez and A Ustarroz. This scheme has at its centre a vast neo-Renaissance Chateau constructed in 1851 around which the winery is created. A lowered central square accessed by visitors from the vineyard is dominated by a monument to the wine grower

'You will never find new lands, you will never find another sea. The City will follow you. You will wander on the same streets and in the same quarters, you will become old; and between the same streets you will grow grey. You will always arrive at this City . For another land you don't wait , there is not a ship, there is not a land.' C P Cavafis. This poem explains the notion of permanence that is linked for ever with the notion of the Classical City.

Renewed interest in our old European cities, that is those that predate the 20th century, has suggest that despite their obvious physical needs, they are the only cities that remain. Study has revealed the complexities of the urban situation and led to the rediscovery of the Idea of the City and reconstruction of its urban disciplines, in contrast with the chaotic reality of our present day cities.

Together with knowledge of the different political, economic and social parameters which determine the City, it is necessary to analyse those issues which, as architects, are the most important for us. It is after all architecture that creates the City, called by Goethe '*Bella Natura* produced by man'. Our interest in the Idea of the City is based on the understanding that it is, a physical and constructed reality. It is neccessary to know the history of a City's conception and construction, to see what it is really like. To return to a discussion specifically on architecture and the City is to adopt a polemic position, especially at a time when people are refusing to see architecture and the Idea of the City as the products of received knowledge. As architects, we should concentrate on one aspect of the City in particular, that is its actual form, leaving out the social or political determinants which characterise other types of analysis. The value of a morphological study of the City lies in the search for objective knowledge of urban events in all epochs and places. Only attentive study of both the imagined and actually constructed forms of the past, can establish the principles of urban discipline, which arise out of experience.

For this, it is necessary to look at the historical development of the European City which had its origins in a continuous accumulation of teachings, that permitted the different elaborations of its characteristic elements. Clearly, the model for the City will always be the City itself, in continuous development of its diverse elements and the relationships that they establish between themselves.

For us, the most important thing, in every city, in its streets, squares and buildings, is everything that can be compared with other streets, squares, buildings or cities, already known. This pleasure of recognition is the basic principle of imitation in the Arts. If as Plato said, knowing consists of remembering, then, the urban discipline consists of recalling knowledge of a well-known City to explain the continuity in all elements and parts. In this way, we can reflect on the process which links the development of the Greek agora with the Roman Forum or with the Main Square. We ourselves use our own experience to recognise and interpret everything about the city.

The Idea of the Classical City was born from laws that ordained its layout, determining the hierarchy of its diverse parts, with the public or the collective dominating the private. This urban idea is neither simplistic not purely automatic. Through the ages, the different elements: monuments, public buildings, housing, streets and squares, have evolved morphological and typological relationships, linking them in subtle and continuous ways, in order to obtain different mixtures, readings and enrichments.

Besides the blend of the Gothic, Renaissance, Baroque City etc that exists in the context of the European City, we can see the development of the street, the square, housing, public buildings and monuments as the component parts of this process. Their developments are assimilated by the Idea of the City, forming part of its history, creating its own logic from within. The City, ancient or modern, has some characteristics that define it forever: the street, the square, the public buildings, the residences, have established between them, through a slow and uninterrupted process, laws of composition. They are as precise as the architectural laws, for example, which define an entablature and its correspondent column.

If such compositional laws are forgotten, as in recent years, the City, deprived of measurement and proportion, corrupts the architectural components within it, creating a monstrous medley which can never be called a true City. That explains why Pausanius said the ancient Greek people refused the name of city for the agglomerations of dwellings which lacked public buildings. If the public spaces, squares and streets are fundamentally unrecognisable, if the public buildings disappear and lose their allotted character, there is nothing of any significance left in the city.

The actual situation that persists in our cities today has been denounced by Walter Benjamin: 'Any thing, any relation, can signify other things. This possibility dictates to the profane world a destructive but just sense: it qualifies it like a world in which it is impossible to reach the detail with rigour.' As opposed to this, Architecture that arises from urban discipline becomes Civic architecture, a public work of art, realised by its material and intellectual permanence. Because of this permanence it is in the City that public spaces, buildings and different architectural styles are best compared to each other.

The knowledge obtained by the comparison, has led to the typological elaboration of architecture which has determined for each building, a specific character, essential and unrenounceable for the creation of a classic City. (The wearisome insistence in all Neo-Classical texts, for example Milizia or Durand, on the idea of the building's character as the principal quality for urban architecture stems from this). If we think, on the other hand, about the composition and the layout of the City, the possibility for comparison can be as far apart in time as Timgad, Montpazier, the Spanish American cities and the enlargements of cities in the 19th century? The survival of logical schemes which remain constant through different epochs, places and cultures contradicts the usual idea that urban structures are just a reaction to the social structures of the time. The whole effect of historic experience on the City, through all its diverse developments, remains faithful to the mechanisms which first constructed this Classical Idea of the City. These are: the limits which define it, the layout that organises its streets and squares, and finally the architecture of its public and private buildings, which constructs and characterises its final image, in dialectic relation with former ones.

The sense of limit, of definition, is inherent in the Classical concept of the City, as it is for architecture. The limit can be understood as a differentiation between two completely diverse realities: the urban constructed reality and the surrounding Nature; or if you like, the artificial and the natural realities. The limits are the best signals of the territory of human intervention, a rational answer to human amazement at Nature. In each moment the existence of limits within the City shows that it is constructed from different and recognisable parts. They do not assume, of course, the impossibility of new enlargements. The City, as its history tells us, can develop new parts which establish new limits, that accord with the initial operation.

The concept of the limit can take different forms, since some are imposed by nature itself (such as rivers, seas, mountains etc) and some are artificially built enclosures – everything from walls to man-made nature, parks, boulevards, promenades with trees etc. It is essential that this sense of limit is recovered in order to end the decomposition and formlessness in the actual city, which invades and destroys the territory around it.

If we require a formal analysis to define the precise form of the city, then there is the orthogonal grid form, as shown by Cities that survive. This represents the creation of a human order amidst the inhuman order of Nature. The orthogonal grid layout is the urban layout most universally applied throughout place and time. It represents the essence of all urban layouts. The combination of rigour and variety which this allows is necessary in the City and in architecture in general. The grid can adapt itself to any possible circumstance. It has been employed in diverse topographies, with widely differing public space formulations, allowing for typological changes.

Although we may think that Alberti's analogy taken from Aristotle, 'The City is a big house and the house is a small City' is merely a beautiful and syncretic saying, there are a lot of evident analogies between the urban project and the architectural project, both the fruit of specific disciplines. Both City and architecture are composed of parts elaborated as their primary elements: streets, squares, public and private buildings for the City, and walls, columns, pilasters, roofs, windows, doors etc for architecture. The analogy is confirmed by treatises on architecture which frequently name urban elements as important parts of the architectural texts and catalogues. For instance, Palladio himself included in his famous *Four Books on Architecture* the restoration of the Roman Square, and Malizia, in the 17th century, considered the streets and squares as a fundamental part of his public buildings catalogue in his *Principi di Archittetura Civile*. We can find the same argument used by Durand in his *Precis* as well as by many other authors.

The City is constructed from architecture, and this naturally becomes urban architecture. The complexity of some of the best architecture reveals its tendency, attested by history , to form cities. The architecture, as soon as it is possible, reproduces *in nuce*, in essence, urban schemes, and the City tends to produce architectural schemes, in memory of man's initial conflict with Nature. Diocletian's Palace in Spalato, or the Escorial by Juan de Herrera, are analogous to cities, syncretic ideas representing the Roman city, or the new Spanish city of 16th-century America respectively. On the other hand, the continuity that was established in a Roman City, between the Forum, grid system, and territory, embodies the unitarian idea of universal order. The most important urban spaces, the street and the square, in every stage of their development, impose their methodological discipline on the architecture built in them, over and above the stylistic variants. Thus, for instance, the medieval street is linkrd with the artisan's house, or the main portico square with the public and private buildings which surround it.

This architecture that is based on the critical knowledge of its own history, like the other Arts, has its origins in the rational imitation of itself. This should be understood as Quatremère de Quincy describes it in his book, *De l'Imitation*, as a rational construction of one image, which searches for resemblance in a previously known and analised object.

Yet, this architecture has no fear of the new, but triumphs in the artistic panorama that dates from Romanticism and carries us to the present avalanche of images of the consumer society. Neither has it any technological fascinations but finds its construction in well known and dominant techniques, conscious of its own limits, heiress of the Greek *techné*. All these qualities originate a necessary and useful beauty. Through this, architecture can explain its origin, permanence and logic as an art constructed and imitated by itself in a continuous process.

However the City and architecture, in our time, have been

rejected because their principles are not subject to the changes of time, because of the continuity of their experience. Men are always after the fascination of a contingent novelty, which follows every technological, plastic and social change. In this way the City and architecture have forgotten their essence and permanence. All these 'novelties' have transported the City and architecture towards progressive loss of identity up to the point of near disappearance.

This recalls the text of Heinrich Gentz, Shinkel's master, who said at the beginning of the 19th century: 'The modern architects believe it is more shameful to imitate a good building, made by a master than it is to make a bad one for themselves. We must think like the Greeks, the Idea, the concept of an Art are more important than the artist himself.' The experience of recent years shows us, that the modern city originating in an architecture of industrial logic, reaches the situation where all its constitutive elements have been sacrificed to only one: the house as a *machine à habiter* accompanied by the car, both of them objects of industrial production.

Under these circumstances the urban spaces, streets and squares do not exist as recognisable in realities themselves. They are simply the remainder when the residential quantity which really constructs the city has been subtracted. The Public Buildings lose their character when collective activity and the urban complexity it evolves are replaced by privatisation, and the equilibrium of the classical city is broken. The intervention of the architecture of industrial logic in the actual historical city has catastrophic results because the heterogeneity of its mechanisms make it impossible to find a coherent resolution of anomalies.

However, when the City and its architecture are the homogeneous result of unitarian and continuous thought, the problems started by the substitution of certain urban elements – city enlargements and the construction of new cities – have been resolved without conflicts.

So every City, every European City is heiress of all the cities which have been constructed in history, appearing as a concrete point in the continuous development in urban activity.

This City, in the Classical tradition, is the only one that interests me, and as a result it is the City which we always want to construct in our projects. This City can only be constructed by architecture of the Classical kind. The City and Architecture must be homogeneous. Our thesis is that every revival of the Idea of the City is accompanied by a revival of the kind of architecture which has made it possible, and vice versa.

Both formulations, architecture and City, are eloquent in certain historical periods, like the Renaissance or the Enlightenment, where the restoration to the discipline of architecture was accompanied by the recuperation of urban classical patterns.

This emphasis on the return, (a characteristic of Classicism, as Thomas Mann tells us in his books), always looks for the recovery of natural and essential patterns from the City and architecture as an alternative to a present which appears chaotic and conscribed by bad taste. Such is a Faustian return, which always presupposes the reconstruction of history, a return to unchangeing primitivity, where man questions himself about the reason for everything which surrounds him. In this sense, the notions of innovation and progress, ancient or modern are only, empty words. As Rilke said, 'Art is an eternal return to beginning'.

The development of the city and its architecture, like that of a civilisation or culture, obeys, as Alberto Savinio tells us, the strict application of a predetermined, inner body of hidden knowledge, where nothing waits upon outside chance, but every variable is anticipated by the whole.

At present, the most important issue for the City and architecture, is the recovery *à la pàge* of certain historical fragments, which curiously enough do revived to replace exhausted repertoires, as in Post-Modernism, but whether a common, durable, essential and Classical architecture can finally construct once more the City, the European City.

The redevelopment of Chateau Pichon-Longueville by M Iniguez and A Ustarroz. Some of the existing buildings on the site were maintained to enhance the sense of history but also so that they could become the focal point of the new architectural development, a reconstruction of a new place where old fragments and new architecture look as if they had been together from the beginning. A two level esplanade has been created with a semi-circular belvedere and several fountains, tiny canals irrigate the square below ending in a large stretch of water at the foot of the Chateau. The most symbolic element of the project where the grape juice becomes wine is highlighted by curved walls suggesting the roundness of the wine vats. The square storerooms are placed at a tangent to the fermentation rooms.

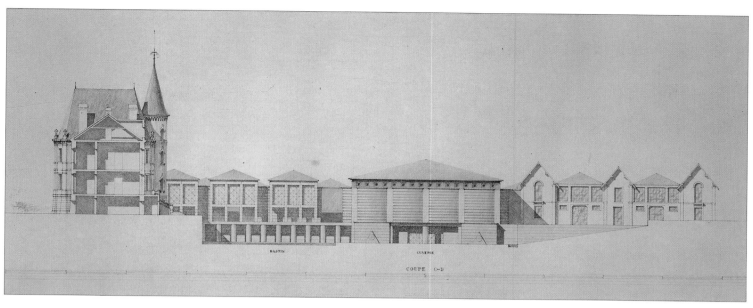

COUPE C-D

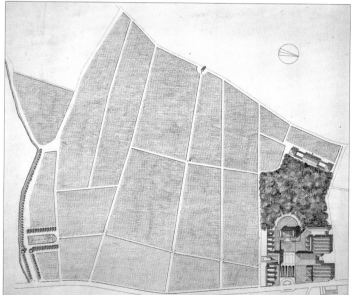

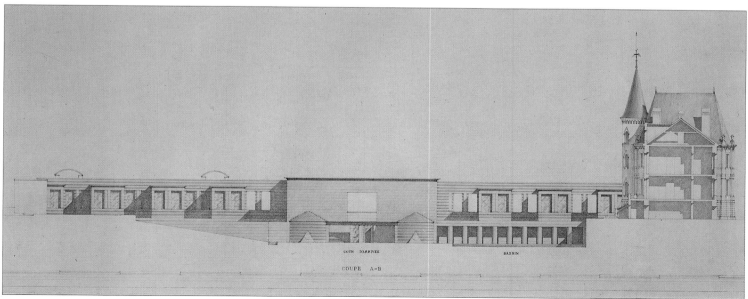

COUPE A-B

Project for the redevelopment of Chateau Pichon-Longueville, Bordeaux, *Above*: Longitudinal site section facing north with the ornamental garden and wall *Centre L to R*: site plan showing relationship of buildings and yards. Ground-floor plan which existing and proposed buildings. *Below*: longitudinal site section facing south through entrance centre and ornamental garden.

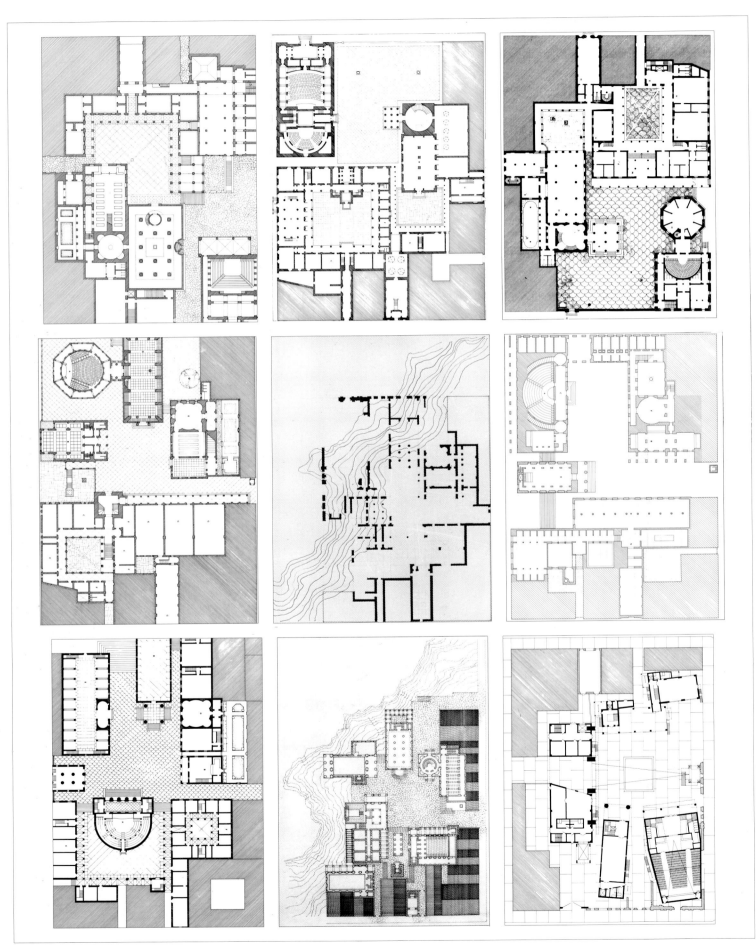

SITE PLANS, *ABOVE L TO R*: C BRITON, N CHAMBERS, L O'CONNOR; *CENTRE L TO R*: L THOMAS, FRAGMENT, L GOODSON; *BELOW L TO R*: M KENNEDY, V DEUPI, M L'ITALIEN

DEMETRI PORPHYRIOS
Institute for the Arts
Graduate Studio at the University of Virginia
Yale University & the Polytechnic of Central London

Nowadays architects are increasingly drawn into public debates about urban design, about conservation and generally debates about an overall awareness of our built and natural environment. Some of them contribute to these discussions happily; others fear that engaging in such discussions might compromise their 'talents' and distract them from their proper concern with architecture as a search for formal originality.

But as the century draws to a close it becomes progressively clear that such debates on urban design and environmental policy are no longer issues that lie outside architecture: They are architecture itself. We can no longer afford to indulge cynically in the destruction of our cities through zoning, traffic engineering or the excremental experience of the strip. For the 20th-century city might work well from the sewers, to the skyscrapers to the strip as long as one considers the wastage in human and natural resources as a concommittant in the sustaining of the overall edifice.

The time-honoured principles of the traditional city constitute today the only body of knowledge that we can look at for guidance. And indeed it is the neglected wisdom of the traditional city – whether European, English, American or otherwise – that is showing fresh signs of life today, at a time when both Modernism and Post-Modernism alike have proven incapable of delivering a socially and ecologically responsible programme of urbanisation.

To architects caught up in Post-Modern Deconstructivist exercises the practical suggestions of the traditional city look not untrue, but beside the point. To them the priority issue on the agenda is the aesthetic heightening of the experience of estrangement that accompanies, so they claim, modern life. But, truly, this is fiddling while Rome burns.

The controversy here is *not* one of stylistics but of design with a view to ecological balance. This is a wholesale programme of re-awakening from controlling the sprawl of our cities, to reconsidering the scale and measure of the urban block, all the way to encouraging a typological understanding of design that establishes hierarchies between public and bread-and-butter buildings, as well as a concern for the civic open spaces of our cities.

As regards architecture proper, plundering the stylistic reservoirs of the past or turning to 'high' technology for an answer will not do. The reasons have been spelled out to us a number of times. We only have to look at 19th-century eclecticism which – much like Post-Modernism – burned out itself for it lacked a fundamental core of experience. Or consider 19th- and 20th-century technology and the effect it had on architecture: with the exception of the light bulb, central heating and plumbing, its contribution to architecture has been minimal. Some might be tempted to add the elevator. But, in truth, the elevator has been an invention that was and still remains irrelevant to the betterment of architecture. The elevator has indeed made possible the high-rise building but the latter has in no way proven a forward step either in terms of quality of habitation or in terms of urban structure.

The same is true for the megastructural developments of the 1960s, recently resurfacing as serious urban renewal contenders in London. Surely, those expansive 'landscrapers' of science fiction must not be counted as a contribution to architecture. As for the so-called 'new' or 'high-tech' materials, we all know too well that not only have they proven utterly unreliable in performance but they have also resisted human domestication. Timber, stone, brick, sheet metal do still today reign as the most reliable and pleasurable building materials.

It is, therefore, instructive that though 20th-century applied science and technology have made unprecedented strides, few of these have been of any consequence to architecture. It is as if technology has 'forgotten' architecture, perhaps in order to tell her that it has long ago reached maturity and perfection and that it should look for no further nourishment from it. Applied science and technology have turned their attention away from architecture towards other fields, like those of medicine, artificial intelligence and genetics.

And so, Brunelleschi's dome cannot be repeated. What I mean here is that the erection of a building which can capture the imagination of its contemporaries because it marks a scientific/technological breakthrough is an experience that belongs to bygone eras. Those who look today at 'high' technology for their clues, formal language or narratives, do not deal with building technology but with gadgetry; that is with a surrogate consumer language, make-believe.

On many occasions in the past, the view I have taken differs principally from those positions. Experience and history tells us that what makes architecture possible, in the first place, is the dialogic relationship between building and architecture. *Architecture makes us see the building craft from which is born, from which it detaches itself as art, and to which is always alludes.* This dialogic relationship between the craft of building and the art of architecture is characteristic of all traditional (that is, non-modernistic) architecture. Of all traditional architecture, Classical architecture best exemplifies this relationship in the tectonics of the Order.

Classical architecture needs also another dialogic relationship: this time the relationship between one building and another. It is for that reason that Classical architecture has no copyright laws. On the contrary, our market ethic of the original and the authentic is based on the pretence that every work of art is an invention singular enough to be patented. As a consequence of this frame of mind, demonstrating the debt of, say, Giulio Romano to Bramante is today called scholarship, but would have to be denounced as plurarism had it been that Giulio Romano was alive. I am afraid that this frame of mind will never allow us develop an architectural culture.

It is unfortunate that it is not only the inexperienced Modern architect who looks for a residual originality as a hallmark of talent. Most of us today tend to think of an architect's real achievement as having nothing to do with the achievement present in that he borrowed. We, therefore, tend to concentrate on peripheral issues of personal stylistics.

But let us think for a moment of the greatness, say, of Alberti. His greatness lies in the fact that he gave a new life to the humanist theme itself which he passed on to the 15th century from the sources of antiquity. The times were different, that technology was different, the politics were different, the *haute-couture* had changed, but the great humanist theme of commodity-firmness-delight was still alive and will stay alive. It is in this sense that we can speak of the Classical as that which endures; but this defiance of time is always experienced as a sort of historical present.

Students were given a fragment of a plan from Letarouilly and were asked to reconstruct it to house an Institute of Arts. A specific brief was given but no context. Initially, students were asked to work within the confines of the urban block without a greater context. This is of course an artificial assumption chosen for didactic purposes; namely, to focus their attention on the typological issues of the individual building and their immediate sourrounding spaces. Once students arrived at an organisational *parti* of the urban block they were then asked to select an urban context within which to situate their scheme. The urban context selected would now be modified so that a dialogic relationship is established between the urban block and the hierarchies of the larger urban fabric.

At the same time in designing their individual building, students were encouraged to reflect on the relationship between building and architecture. To look, that is, at architecture as the symbolic elaboration of the tectonics of shelter.

D. Porphyrios

Students: Christopher H Briton, Nancy N Chambers, Luanne Goodson, Michael B Kennedy, Leslie J Thomas, Victor Deupi, Liam O'Connor, Marc L'Italien

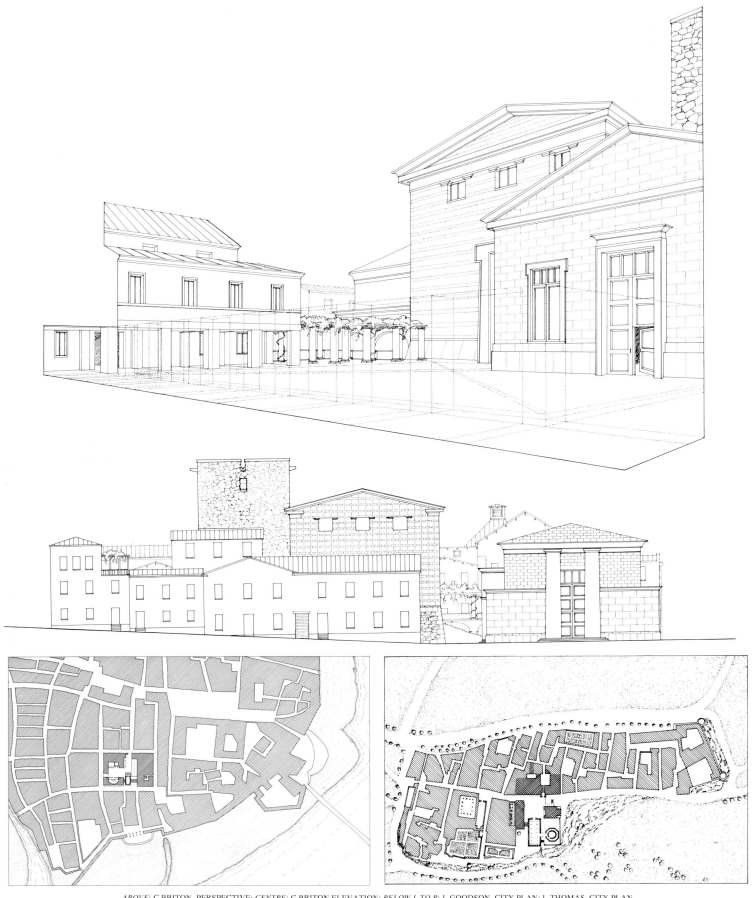

ABOVE: C BRITON, PERSPECTIVE; CENTRE: C BRITON ELEVATION; BELOW L TO R: L GOODSON, CITY PLAN; L THOMAS, CITY PLAN

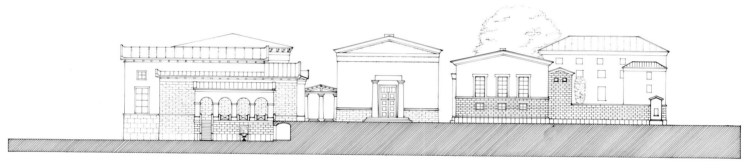

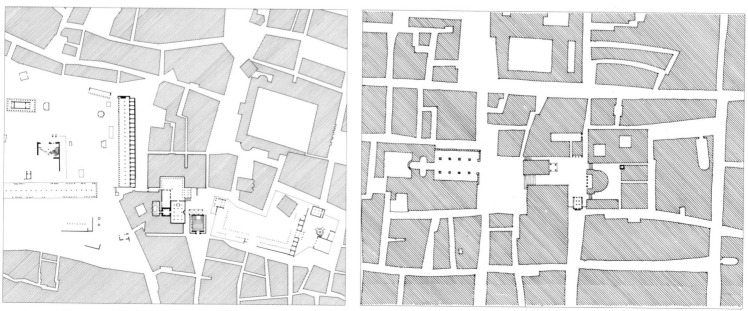

ABOVE: L THOMAS, PERSPECTIVE; *CENTRE*: L THOMAS, ELEVATION; *BELOW L TO R*: C BRITON, CITY PLAN; M KENNEDY, CITY PLAN

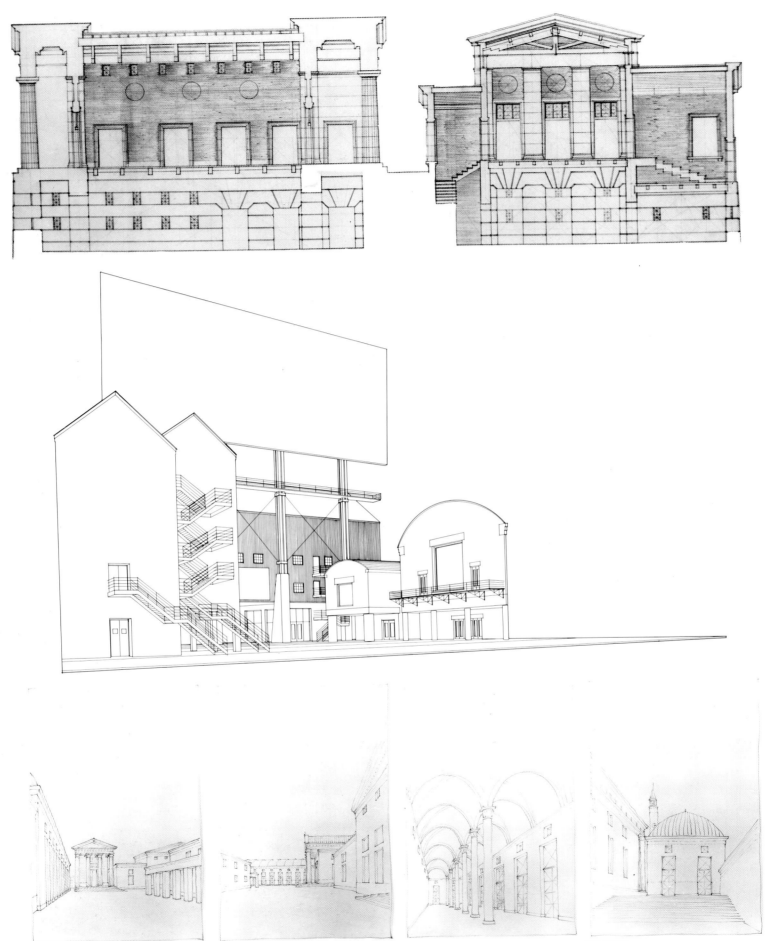

ABOVE: V DEUPI, SECTION AND ELEVATION; *CENTRE*: M L'ITALIEN, PERSPECTIVE; *BELOW*: L GOODSON, PERSPECTIVES